Single and Anxious

Discovering True Contentment and Purpose
through Devotion to Christ

Christina Faith

Single and Anxious

Discovering True Contentment and Purpose
through Devotion to Christ

Christina Faith

Single and Anxious

© 2017 Christina Faith Johnson

NewSeason Books
(in conjunction with Creative Thought Media)
PO Box 1403
Havertown, PA 19083
www.newseasonbooks.com
newseasonbooks@gmail.com

Cover Design by Allen Johnson, Creative Thought Media

All rights reserved. No part of this book may be reproduced in any form or by any means including electronic, mechanical or photocopying or stored in a retrieval system without permission in writing from the publisher except by a reviewer who may quote brief passages to be included in a review.

TABLE OF CONTENTS

INTRODUCTION	1
CHAPTER ONE *You Are Not Alone*	11
CHAPTER TWO *Broken but OK*	27
CHAPTER THREE *While You Are Waiting*	41
CHAPTER FOUR *Eye Candy: How to Live Pure*	53
CHAPTER FIVE *The Promise of Your Singleness*	61
CHAPTER SIX *Building a Heart For God*	79
CHAPTER SEVEN *The Identity Question: Love is Who You Are*	95
CHAPTER EIGHT *Who's the Boss?*	113
CHAPTER NINE *Die Empty*	117

Introduction

Writing has always been hard for me. It is not the actual writing that is difficult though. It's more the belief that people need, desire, or even want to read what I have to write that is mind-boggling. The topic of love, sex, and spirituality is a subject I have too often run away from. As a theologian, I've always wanted to write about the "deep" things of God. However, God has called me to pour out my heart concerning what some people forget is the first step. In order to walk properly before God, you must know who you are and Whose you are. You must know what you are here for and most of all; you must believe that God's plan for your life is perfect.

Nothing in this world tells you the truth about who you are. The world certainly won't tell you that true love is worth the wait. Every song on the radio is about some form of love. One of my closest friends made a comment once that so much of the music on the radio nowadays doesn't even have the word *love* in it. It's all about romance and sex. No wonder the idea of love is so baffling! While most women anxiously desire to be loved, most men anxiously desire to be needed.

I remember my first encounter with the idea of love. I was about 4 or 5 years old and there was a boy who lived in the back of my house. I was so in "love" with him — as much one could be at 4 or 5. He, another girl who lived next door, and myself were all around the same age so we often played together. It was during this time that I should have been learning to have male/female relationships that were built from friendship, but even at this young age, I desired to marry him. I wanted him to be my boyfriend. I wasn't even in kindergarten and I'd already begun to try and meet him at the bus stop when he came home after school. Back then, it was possible to allow your children to play outside by themselves, especially in the rural town we lived in.

In my desire to play with this little boy though, I also desired to express my "love" for him. I found myself doing special *things* for him and we began touching each other sexually in secret. It was also around this time that I believe the seed of sexual perversion was planted. We used to go near the church steps down the street and explore each other's bodies. Of course we had no idea what we were doing, but we'd both seen it somewhere and wanted to try.

I still cannot remember where that sexual experimentation was birthed.

Unfortunately, my family fostered my "liking" him by making little comments about us being together. Thinking it was cute, they constantly encouraged are micro-relationship. They also had no idea about our sneaky visits. They simply aided us in our so-called *love*.

I'm certain that I am not the only one with this story. Many of us were filled with notions and ideas about love as children. And today we see parents and family members planting those premature seeds in children all the time. Because of this, the anxiety to be married or be loved by a significant other is birthed early in adolescence. And this anxiety becomes the same emotion-fueled infatuation that as young adults and adults, we have to fight brutally against in our thought process.

***

Here is my confession: when I got saved (accepted Jesus as my Lord and Savior), I was so jacked up that I clung to every word and anything that could potentially make me better. I then began to force feed what I was learning to everyone in my life. In the long run, I became self-righteous and legalistic. Yes, I,

Christina Faith, am a former Bible thumper. I used to quote Scripture with every word I breathed and as a result, my past is filled with being called fundamentalist, zealot, Jesus Freak, and Christian Superhero. And those were just the ones I heard from other Christians!

Some of this was because of my gifting. I am a natural salesperson. If I like a product, I will try to convince you to love it. After a crazy ten-year, hyper-church experience and two years now of healing, I realize my approach was wrong. I was sharing truth but my application was too much; I was overwhelming.

In 2003, after accepting Jesus, I found myself arguing in a dorm room one day with one of my Hindu friend's roommates. He wasn't a practicing Hindu at the time but he was raised Hindu. I had just finished listening to Ned explain to me his religion. He had a color cartoon-esque chart on his wall of all the Hindu deities and I was genuinely trying to understand how it all worked. I didn't bash him at all. But then he tried to come for my Jesus! Why did he do that? Let's just say we started going back and forth and the argument got heated.

I say all this to say, I won't be arguing scripture with you in this book.

***

I've grown a lot since that day in the dorm room, yet my life is still very much forged by this thing called the Bible. I'll often refer to the Scriptures here. If you are a Christian, great! If you aren't, that's great also! For this book, the Scriptures will serve as the backdrop to my thought patterns and worldview. I wasn't always the person you will read about. At times, changing my heart and mind to think, believe, and act like Jesus has been similar to taming a raging bull.

Yet, there is one area that was different for me. When it comes to how I viewed my singleness, the process was very different. When I came into the faith, I was dealing with 10 (yes, ten!) men at the same time. I was a junior in college and I was feeling myself. I had cultivated a lifestyle of playing games. I was a virgin who tested the boundaries of my curiosities sexually. I'd decided that I would refuse to be in a relationship unless it was going to be serious. In the meantime, I figured that I would go as far as one could without actually being sexually penetrated. My activity of choice? Fellatio.

Real talk, I put myself in some straight questionable positions in my attempt to be a female playa (yes, I just said playa. It was the early '00s). Amongst those 10 guys was one who I'll refer to as the *light-skinned rapper*. I met this guy on an early social media platform called BlackPlanet. I can't remember who inboxed who but I'm not sure I was bold enough to start the conversation back then. But listen, he was *fine!* Not that the others weren't, but this man was super fine. He had this swag about him that made me melt in all the right (well, um, wrong) places. This guy had a mysterious nature to him unlike the others.

He wasn't a great rapper but he *was* a hustler. We spent a lot of time two-waying (hey, it was 2002!) and talking on AIM (AOL Instant Messaging). As all social media hook ups require, we finally decided to meet in person. Our conversation was nothing holy. I decided to invite him over during his lunch break for a snack (before *issasnack* was a thing) and listen…this man gave me the lust-filled snack of all my 21 years. No, I didn't lose my virginity. He never asked for that because we had an unspoken rule. This was just *fun*.

When he left that day, I skipped my class and headed to the studio with one of my friends in south Jersey. When I got out to the car, I was smiling from ear to ear. My friend, we'll call her Badu, said, "Tina, what just happened? You're glowing. What is his name?"

As I explained the who, what, why, and where, we giggled like schoolgirls. Now mind you, I considered myself a G (gangsta). One of my friends would always say, "When Tina falls, it's gonna be hard because she's such a G."

Well, during that lunchtime snack, I had fallen. I made the mistake of falling for the jump off. We spent the next couple months mingling among friends, texting and leaving subliminal messages to each other in our away messages on AIM. At the end of the day though, the light-skinned rapper was poison. I didn't find out his real name and age until I finally asked to see his license. He was definitely not in his twenties.

What I haven't mentioned is, during this time, I also felt God tugging on my heart. I would randomly wake up on Sundays, hung over from a serious night of partying with my girlfriends and have the urge to go to church. After months of running from this urge, I decided to go. During one service in particular, I found myself walking to the altar to give my life to Jesus. My mind kept saying, *Naw, I'm good*, but my feet were walking toward the front. I said the prayer of salvation and they took us to the back room to explain the Gospel to us. When we got there, I made some lame excuse about having to get back to campus for work (I was definitely lying).

I guess going to the back and hearing what I thought would be required of me was too much, too fast. I returned to campus feeling guilty that I'd lied to ministers at the church and had lunch with my friends. When my friends found out I went to church, silence fell over the table and I made some sort of joke to take away the awkwardness of where "Tina, the Sinner" had been.

See, I was certainly not known for anything remotely related to Jesus. My roommate sophomore year gave her life to the Lord and I wanted nothing to do with it. She was my closest friend and I treated her Jesus like a plague. I remember walking into the lounge where they were talking about God and walking right out. I was anti-God and to this day, I am extremely sorry for how I treated her when God was wooing her.

But between the light-skinned rapper and my Jesus experience, everything in my mind was becoming cloudy. I was still messing with the other guys but I wanted only one. I even tried to send him Bible verses but, surprise surprise, he wasn't having it. I wasn't trying to live holy or anything, I just wanted him to come along for the ride. After several attempts to take our jump off status to the next step, he let me know that he wanted to focus only on his music.

Ladies and gentlemen, if anyone gives you the "I'm focusing on..." excuse, know that you will never get what you want from him or her. I was desperately in lust with the light-skinned rapper. I liked him, I really did. But we always want what we can't have and honestly, what we shouldn't have. Looking back at the situation, I was setting myself up for failure anyway. A hook up rarely turns into anything serious and I had a track record of turning down anything that looked like it could be a relationship. I wasn't here for it. However, this was the first time since high school that the other person wasn't here for it and that hurt.

But here's some interesting fruit from that experience: I don't think I'd ever read the Bible so much until the light-skinned rapper rejected me. When I woke up in the morning, I'd read on the toilet. I'd just turn to any page looking for some source of comfort. But, in my mind, none of it was working. So I turned back to partying and wilding out for the rest of the semester. I didn't fail that year, but my grades were the lowest they'd ever been.

That following summer everything changed for me. No one pulled me aside and said, "Young girl you're beautiful. Save yourself." My change came about a little differently. When I got home for break, I contacted one of my other jump offs. This one I met on Yahoo chat. Now if you know anything about Yahoo chat rooms back then, they seemed to be where the real hook ups occurred. The freaks lived on Yahoo chat, which I realize says a lot about me at that time. Anyway, this jump off and I normally just got together on my breaks and it was our routine to reconnect when I got back in town. In truth, this guy wasn't even in my top 5. He was more like a bench rider, but he was always available. I didn't get much excitement out of hanging with him because I thought he was boring. Not to mention that, if I was game, I was sure *he* would take our jump off relationship to the next level. He was old and wanted to settle down. I knew he wasn't for me so I just determined to play along.

One day, I headed over to his house for a "snack" and while there, and rather instantaneously, I finally realized I no longer wanted to live the life I was living. It was like there was a sudden and significant change in my heart.

I didn't know what it meant to live pure but I knew I wanted to find out. On the drive home, I told the Lord, "I won't kiss another man until he's my husband. I am done." Please understand that the idea of living this way was foreign to me. I didn't grow up in church and there weren't any Christians in my life—at least none who were bold enough to confront my hard exterior. I don't know when exactly I ran across the Biblical book *Song of Solomon* but when I did, it gave me the scripture that would be the foundation for the next ten years of my life as a single woman.

"I adjure you, O daughters of Jerusalem (Christ), that you not stir up or awaken love until it pleases." (Sg 8:4, ESV)

***

When I first read that verse it was like water to my soul. I knew I wasn't supposed to be all loose like I was. I wasn't gaming them; I was gaming myself. My heart and body were spread out everywhere and I knew that I needed to change my affections. When you look at the word *love* in this particular verse it is referring to emotional and sexual desire. It is the Hebrew word ʾahăbâh which first means *of man toward man*, then *man toward himself*, next *between man and woman*, and finally, *sexual desire*. [1]

At the time I had no idea what it meant to guide my emotions, but that verse and definition were explicit. Keep them legs closed and them lips off body parts that are not yours by marriage. For some of us, that is harder to do than for others. The raging bull inside of us loves to experience affirmation through sexual affection.

I know, I know. I feel like I can hear your thoughts through these pages. They are the same thoughts I heard my single self say way too often.

"I'm not anxious for a mate at all!"

"This is too hard!"

"But does God really care?"

"Why do I have to wait?"

"How will I know unless I put myself out there?"

OK, I feel you. Like I *really* do feel you. And guess what? God feels you too. I'd encourage you to pray the following verse throughout reading this book: *"Search me, God, and know my heart; Try me and know my anxious thoughts"* (Ps 139:23, NASB).

See, we often put on masks, pretending that that we do not need or want a mate. That, however, is a cover up for the internal longing of our hearts. I never want people to believe that it was smooth sailing living those years as a single woman after opening up the bullpen. It was hard! It wasn't as if I was living in a bubble where fine men weren't all around me. The problem is, they weren't the right men. I knew that God had a special man for me. I didn't want to simply fill my time. I wanted to be pursued by a man who was going to commit to loving, guarding, protecting and watering my heart with the Word of God. I needed a brother who was going to come correct. When God created Adam and Eve he knew that Adam couldn't be alone. He knew that Adam needed a lover. After the fall, there was an attack on the male and female relationship. That attack is still evident today.

There is an all out assault on your singleness. Everything in American culture is telling us to go have sex! Have sex with anyone, wherever you wish! Sex sells, and that marketing of sex pulls us all in. Society has become so callous when it comes sex and love outside of marriage. When Elvis Presley stepped on the scene, they banned the lower half of his body from being aired on television because he popped his hips. Fifty plus years later, you cannot watch television without being sexually engaged with the content on the screen. And hey, I'm not an old maid! I am all for a little kissy face with the characters I create in order to tell the story properly. However, so much of the content nowadays contains full-blown sex scenes that are not healthy for our mental and emotional psyches especially when not positioned in the right context. Combine all that with the fact that, from an early age, we are taught to be in love with the idea of love, and it's a recipe for destruction.

If I told you that your body and emotions were like the Federal Reserve and that only an authorized account holder should be allowed to enter, how would you treat differently that same mind and those same emotions? Why do we care more about protecting our money than we do about guarding our emotions and body?

I once watched an extremely popular R&B/Pop star doing an interview with a well-known radio DJ. During this interview, the DJ asked the singer to rate several female singers and rappers. The singer proceeded to rate the women based on varying degrees of "swag" and "body." Unfortunately, these two men were acting out what many of us see and maybe even do everyday.

We have been trained to determine the worth of those we are interested in by their body and style. Think about all of the people you were interested in over the last year or even your lifetime. What percentage of those individuals were you physically attracted to? Probably most of them, right? But did you really know them from a can of paint, as the elders might say? You simply liked the way they looked. Or maybe they did something you liked? Perhaps, it's the popular "attraction" of today's culture—their abilities. People are obsessed with celebrities, artists, and sports players. If a person can entertain us or perform at a higher level than the average person, we are hooked. Think about high school. The majority of people were attracted to the jocks. I don't know that I've ever seen a group of people praise or lust after the person with the highest SAT scores. And that says something about our human nature.

Here's our starting point: Singleness is about self-discovery and Christ-discovery. It is not about mate discovery. My intention in writing this book is that you would have hope.

What do I mean by hope?

Hope in the Greek is *elpizō*. It means *to be expectant with a joyous anticipation*. I want you to have hope that saving your body is worth the wait. I want you to have hope that God will refine, mold, and shape you during that wait. I want you to hold hope that you can enjoy your singleness to the fullest and use it as a time of healing. Because there is no FOMO (fear of missing out) here. You aren't missing out on anything.

Hope brings an anticipation of blessing in the midst of pain, suffering, and healing. "To know hope, you must endure times of hopelessness. Hope represents an end to desperate longing—a need that begs to be satisfied and in the end is fulfilled. When hope burns within your heart, it cries out to be heard."[2] Lack of hope takes your focus off of His loving-kindness and puts the attention on the current or future despair. This despair causes anxiety. Our hope should always be on God. When God becomes the forethought of our hearts then all of our expectation is on God and not the situation.

When you hope for something, you do it with joy not anxiety. To hope with anxiety is actually not hope at all—that's worry. It is my prayer that you'd learn to wait with joyous contentment in Jesus as He reveals Himself to you and reveals the purpose of your singleness. Let's be clear: Having hope doesn't mean that trials, devastation, and suffering won't happen. Often it's in those times of hopelessness and suffering that God will show you the joy of having hope in Him. It's about discovering joy in the midst of the wait. (see Ps 147:11).

Through my life experiences and examining the lives of believing and non-believing single men and women, I have come to understand that we all have found ourselves struggling with guilt and anxiety in some way. It may be expressed in a myriad of ways, but it's there. The content in this book is for those who are anxious about being married and/or those who've given up on being married. It is my desire to help you walk through the hidden areas of your life before entering into a relationship or while in one.

This book is about striking through the word ~~anxious~~. *Single and Anxious,* the web series, reveals how anxiety can play out in relationships and friendships. *Single and Anxious,* the book, is the antidote to the real life problems reflected in the series. As men and women, we are extremely quick to open the doors of our heart and expose our sexual beauty. We often force it when love is not ready to be awakened. I'm sharing part of my story, the beginning of my journey, because it is my desire that this book will aid you in keeping the doors of your heart and bodies closed until it is time for them to be opened. There is no need to be anxious in your singleness. Enjoy this time! You will never get it back again. Enjoy the ride of learning how not to be single and anxious.

Chapter One

You Are **Not** Alone

Christ wants us to alter our attitude toward ourselves and take sides with Him against our own self-evaluation.
- Brennan Manning[3]

I went to sleep last night with the anticipation that I would be writing this chapter in the morning. I've gone through this complicated, yet amazing journey of being rejected, wounded, and broken. As I mentioned in the introduction, I received Jesus while I was in college and was far from your perfect person—I'd lived 21 years filled with lies, betrayals, and pride before that. And I say that the journey has been amazing because now, in my mid-30s, I can look back and see how God has used everything for my good. It's quite astonishing to see the woman I am today. For so long, my life was like a backdrop for a flower growing in a war zone. And the sad part is, all of it seemed perfectly normal to me.

In all my years, I could never pinpoint the single thing that caused such anger in my heart. Probably because it was never *one* single thing. Was it that both of my parents were functional addicts? That my father OD'd when I was 9 years old, leaving me fatherless? Was it that I had gone to 13 different schools by the age of 14 and was always the new kid? Was it that I never fit in no matter what I did? It was not one but all these things, I think.

Nevertheless, I hope to use my messy life to demonstrate how arriving at a place of contentment, satisfaction, and purpose in singleness is entirely possible.

I should probably add a disclaimer here: For 10 years of my saved life, I attended a church that I thought was extremely biblical, with people who I thought loved Jesus deeply. I later learned, after years of promptings by the Holy Spirit, family, and friends, that this "church" was actually a Christian cult. Much of my time as a single woman was filled with legalism before I decided to leave that church. But remember my point about God using it all for my good? That is true even in this regard. My experience in that organization now gives me a unique perspective: I know what it means to *fight* to walk fully and completely in the grace of God.

Rejection as a root

Let's go back to the light-skinned rapper for a moment. What I experienced with him was a deep rejection that, at the time, was deeper than even I realized. After that experience, for nearly four years, I simply kept it pushing. I fell deeper in love with Jesus by the day and I was so in the zone for God that I didn't think it was necessary to take time to unpack what I was feeling in that situation.

As I was growing in my faith and falling deeper in love with Jesus, I also discovered the beauty of church boys. When I tell you I could pick a good man, I really could. First, there was the choirboy who I'd messed with off and on before I was saved, but when we were finally on the same page, he flatly turned me down. Then there was the Christian frat brother, followed by the future pastor. Oh I can't forget the Christian politician with the MDIV/MBA! The list went on and on. I had two modes. I was either feeling a Christian dude and immediately attaching their last name to mine or trying to let them down nicely after the date.

Throughout all this time, I had some close relationships with friends that helped to expose some of the residual nastiness in my heart. There was one who would truly reveal myself to myself.

Olivia was a friend who seemed to become my best friend overnight. The thing is, in most scenarios, I am an extreme extrovert. And in the last decade or so, most of my closest friends have tended to be introverts. They say opposites attract, I suppose, and Olivia and I were certainly opposites.

In 2008, I decided to move in with Olivia. It was the first time I'd stepped out on my own, away from my mother. It was the most challenging and purifying experience I'd ever had. I had no job, no money, and no family support system. All I had was Jesus and a desire to love people. I'd left my job as an act of faith, and I moved in with Olivia by faith also.

I certainly did not have to move as fast as I did, but in hindsight, I know Jesus was pushing me to take this leap. Unbeknownst to me, moving in with Olivia would be the best thing that ever happened to me. Our personalities were completely different even beyond our extroverted/introverted dispositions. I struggled with a massive case of pride. She struggled with a massive case of *passive* pride.

We had no idea what the Lord was doing with us.

Here's what we did know: we were two single women living in Philadelphia who loved Jesus and wanted to remain holy. When you're single, it's easy to focus on what you don't have. But in that particular season, God shifted both of our eyes from what we didn't have in companionship to what we did have spiritually in Him and where we needed to be perfected.

When you are friends with someone you tend to see each other in pieces. Before we moved in together, we were inseparable. We saw each other's flaws and prayed for one another. We corrected each other in love and extended grace when wronged. This was all prior to moving in. Within the first month of living with each other, we learned quickly that living with your friend is completely different from being able to go home after spending the night at each other's house.

I'd thought it would be no big deal. My childhood home was a revolving door of my family and friends who had lived with us growing up. I'd even lived with friends in college. But within two months of living together, we learned some things about each other without the buffer being able to go to our separate homes. I learned that Olivia shut down when she wasn't doing well spiritually. I also learned that I felt extremely rejected when she did that. I preferred to talk it out — even scream it out — if necessary. Neither of our approaches was the best way to resolve conflict. Olivia had periods where she wouldn't speak to me for days at a time — including one very long 10-day stretch. That hurt me and caused me to react in the ways in which I was familiar.

See, my mom was a single mother who was and is extremely vocal and funny. If my mother didn't like something you did, she would tell you. She is a sharp-tongued woman and both fortunately and unfortunately, I got that trait from her. I used to speak my mind all the time. I'd also say things at the wrong time with absolutely no filter. But Olivia was the type to hold on to things until she was ready to deal with them. It didn't matter how her silence affected the other person, when she was shut down, that was it. And from that, my rejection issues were revealed. But be clear: those issues with rejection didn't start with Olivia. Oh no, our living together was just the experience to unveil them. My issues went much farther and deeper than that.

When wounds are revealed

The conflict between Olivia and me started over yogurt. I know it sounds crazy. It's always the smallest things, right? When I moved in with Olivia, I made a conscious decision to shop at the stores she shopped at for food so we could split the food bill. Olivia was a nurse and extremely health conscious. But at the time, I was not. It was that whole, opposites attract, thing.

I was a soul food cooking sistah and Olivia had this habit of reading the back of every nutrition label. I hated it! I'd started shopping for my household when I was 11 years old so by the time I was 26, I considered myself a skilled cook and shopper. I never looked at the back of products. For what?! Just clean, cook, and eat was how I got down. And I gave Olivia a lot of slack about it in the beginning.

Our first food shopping experience together was a bit awkward. We both put things in the cart and Olivia schooled me on shopping at Whole Foods (how to find the discounts and what to look for on labels). If you can't pronounce it, don't buy it, was her rule of thumb. When we got home we put all the food away and life was grand. For a while.

Olivia loved her personal space. She needed it desperately. I need room too, but I am also extremely welcoming to people in my space. Two weeks after our shopping trip, I noticed that Olivia was avoiding me and responding to me sharply. At first, I ignored it, but 4 days later I decided to address the tension. I approached Olivia and asked what was wrong and if we needed to talk. As I sat there on her floor, I listened to her explain how she wasn't used to sharing her food—specifically, the yogurt. That was the reason why she'd distanced herself.

I was done! The level of rejection I felt during that 4-day period was deep and to find out it was over some organic yogurt?!

My emotions were all over the place after that. I was outraged but I was also thankful. The yogurt debacle sent me into soul-searching mode where I discovered the source of my rejection. It drove me into a deep and painful place of reflection and much needed healing.

***

When I was 21 years old, I remember being in my dorm room, crying, and asking the Lord to forgive me for not forgiving my father. I'd written him a poem that he would never have the opportunity to read and that poem showed me the residual anger I had. I had no idea that I'd held unforgiveness in my heart toward him but Jesus revealed it.

My father had rejected me. His addiction to money, drugs, women, and alcohol took him away from me at a very young age. He was the biggest drug dealer in South Jersey. He was also majorly addicted to the drugs he distributed. I wasn't terribly close to him because of this. Whenever I went to his house as a child, his sister and mother took care of me. My father was always in and out on a mission to get his next high. I only have one memory of spending a birthday with my father when I turned 7.

Empty Promises

It seems as though bicycles have played a major role in the lessons I would learn in life. I have always loved bike riding to this day. I own a nice road bike that I put plenty of miles on even now. But when I was 9 years old, my father promised to buy me a bike. This was huge! I remember calling my grandmother's house searching for my father so that I could get the bike on the 3rd of the month. My father was a drug addict and he had been approved to receive social security so I knew that he would have the money on the 3rd and that it would be gone by the 5th. As I spoke to my father on the phone, he promised me we could go to Kmart to get this bike. I was pumped. I didn't have many moments with my father so this was big. A few days later, when I didn't get the bike, I was crushed.

My father died of an overdose the day we were supposed to get the bike.

For a very long time, I felt like he would not have died if we'd gone to get the bike. In my mind, I could have saved him by occupying the time he would have spent getting high. It wasn't like I didn't know my father was a drug addict. I was very aware of that. But that day, the wound of rejection was opened and it took 18 years for me to even realize the source of my pain.

I incurred a massive wound of abandonment that day. I didn't realize that this wound was so big until I moved in with Olivia and decided to reflect on why I was feeling what I was feeling in the midst of her silent treatment. Was it Olivia or was it my past that I'd never dealt with? We've all been given the silent treatment in life but how often do we take the time to process our emotions instead of being angry with the person who is silent at the time?

Thinking back, that moment, my father's death, was the most significant moment of rejection and abandonment I can remember. And it was me and Olivia's unhealthy way of dealing with a seemingly minor conflict that allowed me to see just how deep my wounds of rejection and abandonment went.

Not only did this experience reveal my wounds, it became a training ground for what my life would look like in relationship. Shortly into living with each other, I became more aware of God's sovereign grace in using our sinful natures as roommates as a way of sanctifying us and preparing us both for marriage and holy living in community.

A reason for it all

Roommate situations can prepare us for marriage but more importantly, they can aid us in becoming more like Jesus. I could have easily decided not to share food anymore or given Olivia the same silent treatment she gave me. Instead I decided to pray for Olivia and my own heart. If there was one thing I was sure of, it was that if I humbled myself and allowed Jesus to purify me first, then I would be an example to my sister in the Lord. Olivia and my father both rejected me. Rejection has always been around me; it has been a theme in my life in many ways. However, with Olivia, I decided to face the rejection instead of letting it rule my emotions. I wanted the wounds of rejection to be healed and no longer just covered up.

We often ignore the wounds that we have. We cover up our wounds very well. The problem is that we can potentially miss the grace of God when we cover them. Our wounds are for our healing. When we cover our wounds without properly medicating them, they become infected. I was infected. I was infected with the wounds of my past and the Lord wanted to clean me off.

The experience of living with Olivia for those three years shaped my understanding of God's ability to divinely orchestrate opportunities for all of us to be formed into His image. Regardless of your past, we all have wounds. Whether you grew up in a Christian home or a non-believing home, our parents, childhood friends, relatives and/or teachers all have created wounds in our hearts. We are born into sin and therefore, we are all destined to hurt another person. However, Jesus came that we might be healed from those wounds. It was never God's intention for us to live wounded and in shame. Jesus desires to use our brokenness to minister to our hearts and pour oil in our wounds.

The great physician Luke told the story of the Good Samaritan in Luke 10. A man was beat, stripped and robbed by robbers on his way to Jericho. He was left for dead. A priest passed him without stopping. A Levite walked past and did nothing. But the Samaritan stopped and helped the man. The Samaritan felt compassion for the man. The Samaritan paid for the man to have his wounds bandaged and oil poured on them. The Samaritan took care of the man as though he was his family. He knew that the man had been badly injured and was in need of care. The priest and Levite had no compassion on the man. The beaten and wounded man was seen as dirty and contaminated in their cultures. However, the Good Samaritan saw a person in need and came to his rescue.

Jesus is our Good Samaritan.

Jesus sees how we have been beaten, robbed and deeply wounded by this world and pours oil—his anointing and healing—on our wounds. The purpose of oil is to soften the wound while it heals. Imagine a wound healing in our day without an antibiotic cream. The wound could possibly become infected or take forever to heal, if at all.

We need the balm of the Lord Jesus to heal our wounds.

If you're like me, then you have plenty of wounds. I don't have a wound or two. I have thousands of wounds—some of which I am still not even aware. A physical doctor would get tired of patching up all the wounds in my heart. Once one was healed, another would immediately appear. However, Jesus doesn't get tired of healing our wounds. He exposes them because He intends to heal them.

When wounds are revealed, we have a tendency to run and put up defensive walls instead of dealing with them. The exposure of wounds makes us incredibly vulnerable. With Olivia, I wanted my walls to erect like the Great Wall of China. Instead, I tore them down by actively engaging her in love. I made her lunch. I cooked her breakfast. I sent her encouraging messages. I became more aware of my actions and the need to define expectations.

When we are wounded we are extremely susceptible to infection. It is extremely important for us to know that Jesus is not in the business of causing wounds. He is in the business of healing them. In order for healing to take place though, we have to experience discomfort. I have never healed from an injury without experiencing discomfort for a period of time.

More Bikes, More Wounds

When I was 5 years old, I attempted to ride an adult male bike. It wasn't just any old bike; it was my uncle's brand new 10-speed. It was a racing bike with all the bells and whistles. He'd left it outside of the house and it was just calling me. I just knew it was waiting for me to attempt to ride it.

If you don't know, I am short. And at the age of 5, I am sure I was very small. As I mounted this bike, I fell while attempting to pedal. As I fell I scrapped my knee. It was extremely bad. Thinking back on it, I probably needed stitches. As the blood gushed out of my little body, I saw the wound. It was wide open. My grandfather cleaned and patched me up. He also disciplined me for attempting to ride a bike of that size. His correction hurt but I knew it was for my good. As he explained, I was too small.

I would feel the effects of my decision for some time. That wound hurt. During the days afterward, I walked with a limp. The healing process reminded me daily that I had an open wound on my knee. I couldn't play or run up and down the street because the healing hurt.

And so it goes with us. When Jesus begins to heal us, we are in a place of grace. We realize that the things of the past have been holding us back. The wounds have been open for so long that we function as though they are normal. We never realize the full scope of our need for healing, that is, until God decides to place us in a situation to reveal that to us. Living with Olivia revealed my need for healing from the feelings of rejection that I experienced as a child. It exposed that I was wounded and broken and in need of oil to be poured on my wounds. In the beginning of my correction, I was extremely defensive. When Olivia addressed her issues with me, I had to make a conscious decision to not be defensive. At first, she was standoffish to me so I was standoffish toward her. But ultimately, I felt ashamed of how I was acting. I was acting that way because I was hurt. I thought, *how could I have wounds?* I was the overcomer. But in all of my overcoming, I still had wounds I'd never addressed.

I had wounds of rejection, abandonment, and pride. These wounds showed up my entire life in numerous ways. I thought I knew it all. I could be extremely aggressive and would put up defensive walls all the time. In that time, Jesus began to reveal his heart of grace toward me. He revealed the truth of Hebrews 13:5: "*For He Himself has said, 'I will never leave you nor forsake you.'*"

Many of us have been forsaken by people and we have transferred those wounds over to God. When we look at God as a person who has hurt us, we miss the manifestation of our healing. It's not that God can't heal us, but we don't recognize the healing. I thought that Olivia's silence was an indication of her rejection of my friendship. God began to deal with me. He showed me that even when people reject us, He never does.

Wounds and Singleness

During this time living with Olivia, I'd begun to make decisions for myself and follow the plan of God for my life completely. As a single woman pursuing purity, this was major. I honestly wasn't thinking about being in a relationship. I had become so acquainted with my wounds that I was consumed with being broken. It was so important that I understood the sanctifying power of Jesus during this time. Jesus had to be my help in this place of rejection and abandonment that I'd just discovered. If Jesus did not become my help, I would have become a wreck. As I began to let Jesus deal with my wounds of rejection and abandonment, a scripture passage remained ever in the forefront of my heart and mind: *"I will lift up my eyes to the mountains; from where shall my help come? My help comes from the Lord Who made heaven and earth"* (Ps 121:1-2 NASB).

We often turn to everything else to cover up our wounds. If you are reading this book, you are brave. You desire to be a better single and not be anxious for a relationship. The first step to removing the anxiety is establishing our need for help. I needed help and still do today. The psalmist cried out that he needed help and he knew where to look for help: *"Yahweh is the psalmist's helper; he is the Creator of heaven and earth* (see the same phrase in 115:15) *and so has all the power needed to protect the psalmist."*[4] God has all the juice needed to power our healing and protection. Shopping, makeup, food, expensive items, children, relationships—and not even our own commiserating on past hurts and pain—has the power to heal and protect us like Jesus. His healing can be immediate. However, in some cases, it's a process. The word *sanctify* in 1 Thessalonians 5:23 is *hagiázō* which means to make holy; make pure is in the future tense[5]. Our sanctification is past, present and future. If you have accepted Jesus Christ as Lord, He has sanctified our past never to bring it up again. He is sanctifying our present to make us clean in this moment and in the future he will bring the ultimate sanctification during our glorification with him in heaven.

The more I realized my brokenness, the more it began to distance me from the concept of being married. I was fearful and ashamed of my anxiety toward marriage. How could I even think about being a relationship with someone when I hadn't dealt with my issues? I had seen plenty of relationships and marriages broken because of internal wounds that weren't ever healed. When I looked at how I felt and responded to Olivia, I thought about my deep need to heal from my past, before I could even enter into a relationship, let alone marriage. I didn't want to wound and hurt my spouse because I failed to deal with my issues. I knew I wouldn't be perfect but I knew with the power of the Holy Spirit, I had the ability to tackle some of my past issues. I learned quickly with Olivia that friendships will reveal where you are if you let people get close enough. It took a lot of prayer and fasting for me to come to the realization that Jesus knew the plans that He had for me.

Commitment is a thing

All my life, I'd distanced myself from long-term commitments in relationships. I was very strategic to cut ties with guys when they began to desire a commitment. I was afraid of commitment. I was deathly scared of it. In college, I intentionally dated many men so I wouldn't get close to any one of them. When the Lord rocked me with His truth, I had to face these fears head on.

I was set on the fact that I would not enter a relationship until I was being courted and I knew it was the Lord's will. After running from commitment for so long, I realized what had always mattered to me was protection and security. I had seen my mother, and so many of her friends, give everything to men who did not value or protect them. I was scared of being like them. But as a believer, I had to break the cycle of lack of commitment. The more God revealed and sanctified my heart the more I realized I needed the body of

Christ. I could not live a holy and single life without other believers who were on the same mission, and who had the same vision to glorify Jesus with their entire lives.

And frankly, community requires confession. It was extremely hard for me to live inside of community and not be honest about my struggles concerning anxiety. Honestly, God made it nearly impossible. While the Lord was cleaning me off, I'd begun to develop affection toward a male friend. This was not an affection I desired. He was a good friend and I wanted to keep it that way. I began to have dreams about him and I getting married—my mind playing tricks on me. But instead of living with this guilt, I decided to confess my preoccupation to my sisters for accountability and freedom. I didn't confess it to sisters who wanted to encourage the thoughts—you know, the homegirls who cosign your foolishness—but to the ones who encouraged me to fight for my freedom; for my purity of heart and mind. As a single person, I decided that I didn't want to offer the man I would marry in the future, sloppy seconds of my emotions or my body. I wanted my affections and love to be for only one. As time went on, I became free of my feelings for this man. I realized that regardless of my emotions, in that particular season, God was more important. So many women become emotionally involved with men in their minds and hearts—men who God did not intend for them. I won the battle over my emotions and continued to pursue purity, but it surely wasn't the only battle.

Free from Guilt

It was not God's will for me to live in guilt and anxiety as it related to my singleness or my past. It is not God's will for anyone to live in guilt and anxiety. But I should be clear: the anxiety I am referring to isn't clinical. I am not referencing the very real, medical condition by the same name. I'm talking about the anxiety of worry. Worrying about the who, what, why, where, and when of life. It's the excessive concern for our lives instead of trusting Jesus in the process. It's the consistent need to be in a relationship in order to be loved, accepted, and valued.

Everyone has secrets that only the Lord knows. I am here to tell you that Jesus wants to free us from these areas of guilt and shame that bombard our hearts. Jesus despised the guilt that sin placed on humanity. He took the disgrace of guilt, sin and death upon Himself that we should be free. It was Jesus who has removed the disgrace of guilt from our hearts at the cross. We are encouraged by Paul to *"fix our eyes on Jesus, the author and perfecter of faith, who for the joy set before Him endured the cross, despising the shame, and has sat down at the right hand of the throne of God"* (Heb 12:2 NASB). When we live in guilt we carry the weight that Jesus' death was designed to take from us.

Guilt is the result of sin. The Israelites struggled with Jesus being the Messiah and the forgiver of all sins, but we aren't any different from them. We struggle with it as well. The truth that Jesus can remove the condemnation doesn't sink deep into our hearts. We live as though we are responsible for lifting the stains from our hearts of past and present wounds. We need the loving compassion of Jesus to remove the stumbling block of guilt from our lives. Jesus desires to make our past wounds a *"footstool of our feet"* (Ps 110:1 NASB). We don't have to live in them.

When we take refuge in Jesus, we are not put to shame. Thoughts of condemnation will always try to run us away from the Lord and community. It is our responsibility to run to the arms of Jesus when guilt tries to overwhelm us. We are not responsible for the forgiveness of our sins. We *are* responsible to confess our sins and turn away from them. It is the righteousness of Jesus that covers us. The Psalmist cried out, *"In you, O Lord, I have taken refuge; let me never be put to shame; deliver me in your righteousness."*[6] Is that our hearts cry? I know it's mine. I have made it my goal to rid my mind and heart from all condemnation by battling those thoughts with the Word of God.

When condemnation wells up in my soul, I speak back to it with declarations of joy in the Lord. Being overwhelmed by shame, guilt, and condemnation doesn't have to be our daily life. In Jesus, we find an everlasting peace that cannot be taken away from us. I discovered this peace when I learned to meditate on the Word of God in my singleness. My mind used to race with thoughts of condemnation, shame, and guilt. Condemnation and guilt from sins that I had committed and repented of, and shame from things that had been done to me. Early in the morning it seemed that these thoughts would bombard me even more. Thoughts of not being good enough, not reading my Bible enough, not loving enough would rush through my mind. One day I took my mother's advice and tried meditating. Sitting on my floor I took a note pad, pen, and Bible. I kept speaking one verse over and over, *"cast all your anxieties on him, because he cares for you."* (1 Peter 5:7 ESV) When thoughts or things I needed to do that day came to mind I wrote them down and went back to the verse.

Jesus knows the anguish of our souls. He is not afraid to love on us in our pain. It is Jesus who has welcomed our broken hearts into His loving arms. That day, for a moment, while repeating that verse over and over, I experienced the divine peace of God. Will you choose to be glad and rejoice in His love, for He sees your affliction and knows the anguish of your soul? (see Ps 31:7 NIV)

As we move forward, I encourage you not to shrink back into the despair when God highlights areas of weakness like I did when the Lord revealed my issues of rejection and abandonment over some yogurt. Remember the Lord is here to pour oil in our wounds and show mercy to us. He doesn't do this by Himself. He uses His disciples—our fellow believers--to do it. As God heals our wounds, we are then called to pour oil on the next person's. That's how we know we are not alone in this. At all.

AN EXERCISE IN REFLECTION

Before we move any further I want you to write down what you are ashamed of and what anxiety about that shame, sits on your heart.

_____

_____

_____

_____

_____

_____

After you have written down your list, write next to each entry, one of the the following sentences:
- Jesus, forgive my shame.
- Jesus, cover my sin.
- Jesus, release me from guilt and shame.
- Jesus, make me righteous.

A Prayer

Jesus, you are amazing and beautiful. Wounds of shame that have caused anxiety have covered me, and I am handing those wounds over to you, the Great Healer. Help me be brave and courageous while you reveal those hidden wounds of my heart. Pour oil on my wounds and heal me from the inside out. In Jesus' name, Amen.

Chapter Two

Broken and OK

"I am broken and it's OK."

These were the most revolutionary words I'd ever heard. After being in the Lord for 5 or more years, I had become accustomed to understanding that I was broken. I was so hard on myself and I took correction extremely hard. I took corrections personally, as most of us do, without any understanding that it was Jesus showing me that He loved me and wanted me to reflect His image. Those who know me know I have an extremely big mouth. As I said, I am an extrovert. Most times, I say what I am thinking and feeling and that has gotten me in much trouble over the years. Even when what I am saying is good and could be beneficial, I've often said it with pride or out of order. I didn't have a filter for other people's feelings. This was one of the hardest things for me to understand. I hadn't taken much of a watch over my words throughout my life. I suppose I get that from my mother.

Needless to say, I was very aware of my brokenness.

For 10 years I served in a community of people who were extremely legalistic and that legalism often showed up in the correction they gave. Instead of being lovingly corrected, I was often corrected harshly and, many times, in public. Honestly, this didn't help with my harsh tongue. While under this leadership, I thought that correction should always be "straight with no chaser." After receiving one of the more brutal "correction" sessions, I found myself experiencing a gruesome amount of guilt and shame about my pride and how it kept getting me in trouble. I had fasted, prayed, studied for years for pride to be broken off of my heart but it kept showing its evil head. I was tired of it! I sat on my bed and listened to a podcast by Laura Hackett (Park) and she spoke about the Lord revealing to her that she was broken and it was okay. I can't tell you what else she said that day but I know that it was that phrase that resonated with me.

I was broken and it was okay.

God hadn't turned his back on me because of my struggle. He was displeased with my pride, sure. He continually tells us in His love letter called the Bible that He hates pride. We see the Father's hatred of pride in Proverbs: *"The fear of the Lord is to hate evil; Pride and arrogance and the evil way. And the perverted mouth, I hate…"* (Prov. 8:13 NASB). It wasn't okay that I had lived in pride. But it was okay that I was broken. I was broken but He still loved me.

What I discovered through my brokenness is that I too often failed to accept the grace I was given because I only saw the sin of pride and had only been given the truth of my pride in correction without love. I had to learn how to receive the grace that God poured out. "You have not received grace, so how can you give it to others? And as you feel tormented, you hurt others. You've got to collect on the grievances, collect on your hurts. [7]

I'd been extremely harsh to others and myself and that needed to change. I need to be change from the inside out—not by harsh correction but through the loving hand of God.

God is hurt when we sin but that is why He sent Jesus. Jesus is our ocean of grace. Jesus is the Lover of our souls that takes the things God hates and washes them with His blood. When Jesus died, He didn't just die for our past sins. He died for every sin we would ever commit. Being okay certainly doesn't mean that we settle in our sin. It means when God exposes our flaws, we don't focus on them; we keep our eyes on Him and cry out for that healing. Jesus is not okay with us remaining the same people that we were when we got saved. He is not okay with us being the same person we were yesterday. He has given us grace to be sanctified daily.

I can remember it clear as day. I was lying on the bed in our two bedroom, "single ladies" apartment. My heart was aching. It was aching that I was still struggling with the same sin. I was struggling with the anxiety of carrying my pride into marriage and passing it down to my children. It was a deep issue in my heart and I saw no light at the end of the tunnel. I felt broken and being okay with that brokenness was never a thought. In my mind, I needed to fix the problem. The problem was sin and I had continually used my mouth as a weapon.

Your struggle may not be pride. It might be something else. And maybe you also can't see any light at the end of your tunnel. I promise there is a way of hope out of tunnel.

You are broken and it's OK.

That day, Laura's words resonated and it gave me the courage to accept my brokenness. I tell people all the time that your singleness is the greatest time of your life to allow the Lord to work on your heart issues. I didn't have to rush to get myself together that day. I laid there on the floor weeping but my tears were not shed because of my brokenness but because of the grace God extended to me. He wasn't angry with me. He was in love with me. His love desired to make me more like Him and in that process I discovered a portion of my heart that needed deep healing. Instead of beating myself up I reminded myself of Romans 5:20, *"where sin abounds grace abounds more."* His grace is made available because we are broken. Often in our singleness we focus a lot of attention on what we aren't and where we aren't. Yet God desires us to focus our attention on who He is.

Shine Bright Like a Diamond

"So, as those who have been chosen of God, holy and beloved, put on a heart of compassion, kindness, humility, gentleness and patience (Col 3:20)

Jesus chose us and therefore we are holy. Period. Often we complicate the word "holy." Being holy doesn't mean you watch G-rated movies, listen to only Christian music, and are a hermit. Holiness is being set apart because of Jesus, not because of your works. Bob Goff is an incredible author who writes and speaks about love. He stated, "Watch out for people who act holy but don't get their holiness from Jesus but from the stuff they've done, which is pure delusion."[8] We don't make ourselves holy even though, sometimes, that's how we live. The truth is, we can't do anything good without Jesus and we surely can't live holy lives with Him. We are broken and it's okay but we don't stay broken.

If I could speak to my younger Christian self, I would tell her not to think that her actions make her holy or like Jesus. There was a time when I was the delusional Christian who threw away her CDs, DVDs, and stopped talking to non-believing friends.

Whew! That pride is an absolute beast.

But I was following the teaching I was exposed to. There were many teachings during this time about the secular world and Christians being sure to remain holy and "set apart." To this day, I shake my head at the fact that I got rid of over 500 DVDs and CDs because of legalistic teaching that had nothing do with what it means to be truly holy. It was so bad, and hilarious in hindsight, that the garbage man knocked on our back door to say thank you for the come up.

The delusion of self-made holiness is that God is pleased when we remain separate from what we perceive as *evil*. We're certainly responsible for fleeing from evil things that pervert the holiness that He has placed on us (2 Ti 2:21 NASB). But what someone should have told me was take a break from consuming nothing but entertainment. They should have said, take a break from some of your friends headed in another direction or simply have a talk with them about the change in your heart. Instead, I became the super Christian and that offended a lot of people.

When I first created the character *Sebastian* in the *Single and Anxious* web series, I was very intentional about him being the only Christian among his friends. Sebastian has real life problems and emotions. I wanted Sebastian to deal with those problems out in the open. We don't see him go to church every episode. We see a young man with problems whose only difference is in how he handles those problems. Holiness isn't being perfect; it's being set apart because Jesus sets us apart for His use.

Recently, I've been marveling over the understanding that we are made just—despite our guilt. We don't deserve to be justified but that is the amazing character of God. He loves us when we are unlovable. We are guilty of sin yet we are forgiven. If you are struggling with the weight of guilt from not measuring up to the standard of holiness, there is an incredible ocean of grace waiting for you right now.

It's God's desire for you to shine like a diamond but in order for us diamonds to shine, he has to first clean us off. Struggling with sin isn't a sin. It's a part of the process. The Holy Spirit is our Helper and Comforter so we aren't left without hope (see John 14:26 NASB). We will live with Him eternally and it's not because of any work that we ourselves have done. We are justified by the blood of the Lamb. Jesus didn't deserve one lash that He received. He didn't deserve any of it, yet He willingly laid down His life to cover my pride. My lies. My hate. Our coveting. Our lack of hope. Our lack of faith. The amazing truth of the love of Jesus is that He did it once and would do it again.

> *But now apart from the Law the righteousness of God has been manifested, being witnessed by the Law and the Prophets, even the righteousness of God through faith in Jesus Christ for all those who believe; for there is no distinction; for all have sinned and fall short of the glory of*

> *God being justified as a gift by His grace through the redemption which is in Christ Jesus; whom God displayed publicly as a propitiation in His blood through faith. This was to demonstrate His righteousness, because in the forbearance of God He passed over the sins previously committed; for the demonstration, I say, of His righteousness at the present time, so that He would be just and the justifier of the one who has faith in Jesus (Ro 3:21-26 NASB).*

So being broken isn't the problem. Choosing to give up when He shows us who we are, is. I was anxious to be changed. I should have been humbled that He was showing me that He loved me. God corrects those He loves. Imagine a parent that never corrects their child. That child would look like an orphan who is not cared for in any way.

And so it is with us. It is His discipline that allows us to be more like Him. Let's pause for a second and consider what loving discipline looks like as a single person. When we mention the word discipline, folks get out of hand. I was one of those folks. When I was single, I had a few friends who were dating (courting) each other and I discovered that they had been with each other alone at her apartment. With this information, the loving way to handle this situation might have been to ask my friend if she wanted my feedback about the dangers of being alone with a man she was extremely attracted to while they were both waiting for marriage to have sex. Instead, I went full throttle legalist on her. In an effort to "discipline" her in the area of avoiding the appearance of evil, I *told* her she was in sin and that should have never happened. Because I didn't approach the situation in love, the "discipline" turned to judgment. My friend was already feeling horrible about being alone with him so I added to her anxiety and guilt. In learning how to become content in our singleness, yes we have to address the issue of avoiding compromising situations.

However, God's discipline shouldn't lead to feeling guilty and ashamed. We share in His holiness when He disciplines us. When we begin to understand that discipline is love and not anger, we will be able to accept more of the grace He sits at the table for us (see Heb. 12:10 NASB). God is faithfully perfecting us and building us into better reflections of Him (Phil. 1:6 NASB). God will discipline us and He will use others to discipline us in our singleness but it should be done in love. Discipline should lead our hearts to draw closer to Him in singleness not make us want to run the other direction.

Embracing Our Brokenness

Jesus loves us so much that He is not willing to leave us in the state that we are in. Jesus desires that we live broken lives. We aren't broken by sin and death anymore. Sin no longer has control over us. We are those who have the power of the living God inside of us to reject sin. When we sin, we are now able to repent and turn from that sin. But to fully be willing to turn, we need to live broken lives before God. "To be broken means to have no rights before God and man. It does not mean merely surrendering my rights to Him but rather recognizing that I haven't any, except to deserve hell. It means just being nothing and having nothing that I call my own, neither time, money, possessions nor position.[9]" That is hard for us to do.

If you are anything like me, when I first discovered what brokenness meant, I just knew that I wasn't broken. I was so wrong though. Much of my old self still existed and, if I'm honest, still exists to this day. We are supposed to be dead to ourselves. However, the old man inside of us rises far too often. Scripture says, *"For you have died and your life is hidden with Christ in God. When Christ, who is our life, is revealed, then you also will be revealed with Him in glory. Therefore consider the members of your earthly body as dead to immorality, impurity, passion, evil desire, and greed, which amounts to idolatry* (Col 3:3–5 NIV)." We are broken and flawed human beings who are given the opportunity to be broken by the power of God.

There is no need for us to defend ourselves when we walk in brokenness. Extending grace is in God's DNA. He is love and that love is expressed through the awesome nature of His truth. Let us not fall astray in this life. Let our hearts desire reflect His DNA. God can be trusted with our brokenness. When we surrender our wills to His He molds us into His image. Our lips begin to have His shape. Our mouths are full of love, grace, truth, hope, mercy, and truth. Our eyes take on His slants. They only desire to see beauty, purity, grace, and faith. Our ears are shaped like His. They are full of good things, they listen closely before thinking, they are protected against gossip and slander, and they only hear what He says.

Brokenness requires a deep well of humility. We can't be broken and molded into His image if we are not humble. God can't use a prideful person. He can't mold and shape us when we are prideful because we are stiff. There is a well that is available to us to enter into His courts. When we turn our hearts toward being thankful for what God has done, we can humble ourselves in prayer. My introduction to being broken was birthed in a place of prayer and desire for humility. "Humility is essential if we desire to pray with authority. Humility means agreeing with God about who we are and what we can do. Humility eliminates the idea that we tell God what to do[10]. When we are walking in our brokenness, we want to hear what God has to say. We are not fighting the Holy Spirit to do things our way. We are fighting our selfish nature to do what we are told by the Holy Spirit. Our fight is well worth it because we are then able to walk by faith because we trust God.

Have you ever heard someone talking about provision? We often speak about provision in regards to earthly things but God looks at provision concerning EVERY part of our lives. We must continue to remind ourselves that *"no good thing does He withhold from me* (Ps 84:11. NIV)." When we bow before the King in humility we can expect nothing but goodness to spill out of Him. We can walk by faith and trust Him because He is good. Singleness isn't a curse of loneliness, it's the gift of time to learn how to walk by faith and allow Him to clean you off.

God: Come and Talk to Me

What is your prayer life like? Is it dry, brittle, unexciting, non-existent, or a task? I have been in that place before. At times, I felt like I couldn't even open my mouth. The enemy had me so confused as to why I needed Jesus. Did He hear me when I prayed? Was His delay a no? Was I His child? Was I waiting for Him in vain? All of these questions caused my prayer life to become dull and brittle. It created a lack of urgency.

Brokenness hurts but it's rewarding. It creates a daily urgency in our hearts for more of God and less of us. When we are broken we are exposed to our wounds, flaws and issues. But when we are broken, God gives us a sense of hope. Hope that He does hear us. Hope that we are His children. Hope that we do have authority in Him. Hope that we are accepted into His love. Hope that He walks with us. Hope that He is right there with us molding and shaping us; putting water and oil on His hands as the Potter's wheel spins to smooth out our rough edges.

Being broken doesn't have to create a negative effect on our lives. Too often we run from our wounds and allow satan to have a foothold in our hearts. "Lack of urgency in prayer gives Satan the foothold he needs to completely demoralize and despiritualize our prayer lives.[11]" We need the grace of God. We lose out on what the Lord has for us when we despiritualize our wounds. Grace is available in abundance regardless of the situation. God is dedicated to showing us His grace. His loving-kindness is His loyalty and determination to suffer long with us in love until we come to Him broken and needy.

The apostle Paul understood the pain of wounds and weaknesses. He had a weakness that He cried out to the Lord for repeatedly. I am sure Paul felt at times that this weakness would always get the best of him. In the midst of his pain, Jesus graciously poured oil on his wounds to the point where

Paul desired to boast in his weakness. Let's look at some of the exchange:

> *And He has said to me, "My grace is sufficient for you, for power is perfected in weakness." Most gladly, therefore, I will rather boast about my weaknesses, so that the power of Christ may dwell in me (2 Co 12:9 NASB).*

God doesn't look at our weakness as a slave master would. A slave master looks at your weaknesses and says that you are despicable or that you are a liability. God looks at our weaknesses as a husband. And before you go there, God isn't the average husband. He's the perfect husband. He is our greatest example of what it is like to be loved rightly as a single. Whether you're a male or female, God is our husband. In our singleness, we may not have a natural spouse but we sure do have a spiritual spouse. As our husband, He teaches men how to love a woman like God loves His church and He teaches woman how to love her future husband back (Eph. 5:25 ESV). If you want to prepare for marriage, continually talk to your spiritual Husband about your relationship with Him. Your relationship with God. He is the one who will suffer long with you in your weakness. He washes you with the water of the Word to sanctify you as a husband should. The word *grace* here is χάρις or cháris. We have often heard grace described as undeserved favor and that is true. However, it is more than that. Grace has a depth that turns our mourning into joy. As Paul struggled with his wounds, he heard the Lord speak grace over Him. The word grace here is particularly that which causes joy, pleasure, gratification, favor, acceptance, for a kindness granted or desired, a benefit, thanks, and gratitude.[12]

Paul was able to boast because He took pleasure in his pain. He knew that He didn't deserve the grace of God. God did us an undeserved favor when He gave us grace. Grace isn't given by our works but by His. We are able to walk empowered in our weaknesses because He is perfecting us.

Jesus is intimately acquainted with the emotions that we experience on a daily basis. Instead of casting us away He draws us closer into a deeper brokenness and dependence on Him (Ps 147:5 NASB). He is strong enough to carry every one of our burdens.

Trigger alert: When I was growing up, I unknowingly made a huge mistake. I hid my heart. The first time I remember hiding what was going on with me was when I was 7 years old. My mother's friend's son was sexually abusing me. He was supposed to be watching me while they were out. I didn't tell anyone until I was in the 7th grade when I wrote a letter to my friend telling her. He did threaten to hurt me if I told but I don't know if it was the fear of him that scared me or if it was the fear of feeling like I did something wrong. I thought I was the reason for us watching a porno while our parents were away. My mother didn't find out about the abuse until I was 25 years old. I'd written a letter to my abuser explaining that I had received Jesus into my heart and that I had forgiven him. Unfortunately, I didn't have all the correct information and it was returned to sender and my mother read it. I don't know if I didn't tell her earlier because I didn't think that my mother was strong enough to carry both my burdens and her own. Those were always my questions: Was my mother strong enough? Could I share my heart with her? As an adult, I know now that I could have most certainly told her about the incident and anything else that I was going through. I now understand that by hiding the abuse it created a need in me to never want to feel that vulnerable again.

I understand now that could have talked with my mother but I often refuse to apply that same logic to the rest of my life. I am a child in need to the Lord and so are you. Our need is expressed by our continued weaknesses so our need for Him is deep. He asks for our burdens. He asks that we cast the whole of care on Him. He asks that we receive His grace. But do we? Are we vulnerable with the Lord? Before I could be vulnerable with anyone else, I had to learn how to first be vulnerable with the greatest Lover of all time. If I had not accepted the invitation to talk to the Lord in my singleness, I would not have been able to be vulnerable in my relationships. Being single is not easy in the 21st century. Everything is telling you to be strong and independent. But God is asking for our hands in this life. He desires for us to take His hand and allow Him to be mighty, bold, strong, and full of love.

    He is abundant in strength. We aren't dealing with a weak self-made God who turns away from us when we disappoint him. We are dealing with the Rock of Ages (see 2 Sa 22:3–4 NASB) who beckons us to come closer for renewal and renovation of our entire beings. Take a second and think about who or what you run to when you feel broken. That person or thing is your way of coping, you know. God wants that thing or person's place. God wants to be your rock.

> *My God, my rock, in whom I take refuge,*
> *My shield and the horn of my salvation, my stronghold and my refuge;*
> *My savior, You save me from violence.*
> *I call upon the Lord, who is worthy to be praised,*
> *And I am saved from my enemies*
> (2 Sam. 22:3–4, NASB).

    When God can satisfy us in our pain, we are delighting in Him. He can then be our rock. He can be our refuge. He can be our shield. He can be our safe place. He has all that we need in our brokenness. He is most glorified in us when we are most satisfied in Him.[13]

AN EXERCISE IN REFLECTION

Before we move any further I want you to write down some areas of holiness that you struggle with and areas you can be vulnerable in God

_____

_____

_____

_____

_____

_____

_____

After you have made your list, write next to each one of those struggles, the following sentences:

- Jesus, I trust You.
- Jesus, help me talk to You about my weaknesses
- Jesus, give me the courage to open up to You.
- Jesus, help me to forgive myself.

A Prayer

Jesus, so many areas of weaknesses and wounds were revealed reading this chapter and in a lot of ways, I have no idea what to do with that. But Lord, I want to trust You with my whole heart. I want to be holy like You. I want to be vulnerable with You. I want to hear you speak to me. I want to heal from the wounds from the past. Can you give me the courage to let you into my life in a big way? Help me confide in You. In Jesus' name, Amen.

Chapter Three

While You Are Waiting

Sitting on the couch with my friend Gina, I listened to her explain her frustration with her new relationship. Gina and Mark had been dating for 6 months and they were already talking about marriage. Now some people may be blessed with those sparks immediately but those sparks were not there for Gina and Mark. Gina's expectations were way too high from the start of their relationship. This—for most people—is not uncommon. With every relationship, even with God, you need to talk about expectations. God has certain expectations of you and He outlines what we can expect of Him. Think about your expectations of God. Do you expect Him to make you whole? Do you expect for Him to provide your spouse at the right time? Do you trust Him that much? Trust is a major part of all of our walks with God no matter our marital status. The deeper the well of trust in your singleness, the better you will be prepared for the trials of learning to trust God in your marriage. Abraham is known as the *father of the faith*, however, before he walked in that faith, the Lord exposed his trust issues on numerous occasions. Remember the Abraham, Sarah, Hagar debacle? Abraham and his wife, Sarah, were barren and couldn't have children. In

Genesis 12:1-3, God gave Abraham a promise that Abraham would father many nations. In Abraham's mind, this wasn't possible because Sarah was barren and they were already 75 years old, but they followed the Lord and left their home land of Harren.

When we initially hear the Lord speak to us about a promise, we often believe superficially. We believe just enough to take the first step of faith. Abraham and Sarah took the first step of faith and left town. But they didn't fully follow the instructions. God told them to leave their family behind. They did not.

Several verses down the line Abraham, Sarah and Lot went to Egypt for food for there was a famine in the land.

> *It came about when he came near to Egypt, that he said to Sarai his wife, "See now, know that you are a beautiful woman; and when the Egyptians see you, they will say, 'This is his wife'; and they will kill me, but they will let you live. "Please say that you are my sister so that it may go well with me because of you, and that I may live on account of you"* (Gen. 12:11-13 NASB)

Sarai must have been an extremely gorgeous woman because as soon as Pharaoh's official saw her, they took her to Pharaoh the king. He immediately wanted to take her on as his wife. Abraham knew his wife was fly! He knew that she was a prized possession that men would kill for. Logically speaking, he did the right thing in his natural mind to protect himself. However, the Lord didn't allow Abraham to live in his lie. His lie was immediately exposed. God was gracious to Abraham by plaguing Pharaoh for taking Sarah on as his wife.

> *But the Lord struck Pharaoh and his house with great plagues because of Sarai, Abram's wife. Then Pharaoh called Abram and said, "What is this you have done to me? Why did you not tell me that she was your wife?*
> *"Why did you say, 'She is my sister,' so that I took her for my wife? Now then, here is your wife, take her and go." Pharaoh commanded his men concerning him; and*

they escorted him away, with his wife and all that belonged to him (Gen 12:17–20 NASB).

The Lord is our shield in the midst of our muddy waiting (Gen 15:1 NASB). Abraham made a mistake in not trusting God to be His shield and provider several times. He lied about Sarah being his wife twice, he brought Lot with him, he slept with Hagar, the servant and had a child, and scoffed at God when He promised him a son from Sarah at 90 years old.

But just like Abraham, sometimes we move out of order. My friends Gina and Mark certainly did. Before they spoke about marriage, they should have set their expectations for developing their friendship. Doing so would have given them time to see if marriage was in their future.

Sometimes we put the cart before the horse in hopes of protecting the cart — not realizing that the horse has to pull the cart for it to move, Instead of fully listening to the Lord, Abraham took his nephew Lot with them. He was disobedient. While we are waiting, do we follow in complete obedience to the Lord? I know that I don't always. When things seem hard or look like it will be a problem, how do we respond?

God still has a plan

Abraham made a lot of mistakes but God didn't turn His back on him. He had major plans for Abraham and his descendants. While we are waiting we have to keep our focus off of the "how." We don't always see *how* God is going to do what He promised or *how* he's going to bless us with what we desire. But we must trust that He will do it. Because here is the hard truth: God is more concerned with *how* we wait rather than the length of our wait.

But do not let this one fact escape your notice, beloved, that with the Lord one day is like a thousand years, and a thousand years like one day. The Lord is not slow about His promise, as some count slowness, but is patient toward you, not wishing for any to perish but for all to come to repentance (2 Pet. 3:8–9 NASB).

God doesn't see time like we see it. For example, I've been asking my husband to install a clock in our bedroom for a few months. He was very apprehensive to put this clock up. I got in the bed after a long night and I saw the clock. I was ecstatic about the clock. I can now look up and see what time it is instead of depending on my iPhone. However, I began to see why he didn't want to install the clock. A clock with hands has seconds and we can hear every single second that ticks. It's a recipe for anxiety-ridden sleep.

Well, isn't that just like us when we are single? While we are waiting, we tend to only hear the seconds ticking and we become extremely anxious. We literally can hear time passing. But God doesn't even consider the seconds, minutes, hours or days that we live by. He doesn't operate by our earthly time and date system. Peter explains to us that God's sees our thousand years as a day. That is mind blowing. Jesus died and rose for our sins over 2000 years ago yet in God's mind it is only two days? When we think about God's promises toward us, we have to consider that He *rarely* gives us what He ultimately desires immediately. Scripture says, *"But do not forget this one thing, dear friends: With the Lord a day is like a thousand years, and a thousand years are like a day"* (2 Peter 3:8 NIV). God isn't a genie that we ask for something and He immediately gives it to us. His giving is always a part of His purpose and plans. If you're anything like me in those times of waiting in line for God's *yes, no or wait longer*, you are always challenged. But I must admit that it's in those times that I discover more wounds and broken. I uncover that I am not as grounded in faith as I imagine. Think about what it would mean to give a 10-year-old child their inheritance. They would likely spend it on candy and video games. We are the same way. If God did not build waiting into our experience of Him, we would waste what He intends to use to bless us.

Abraham had a lot of opportunities to fail before God provided Isaac as his inheritance. He failed over and over in the areas related to his trust and faith in God. However, he continued to believe, even when life was unbelievable.

Abraham is the father of the faith. By faith Abraham offered Isaac as an offering to the Lord to be slaughtered. If Abraham had not failed over and over, I doubt he would have had the trust to believe that God would provide an animal for his offering when God called him to use Isaac.

Can you trust God enough to offer your marital status as a sacrificial offering to Him? If you never get married, will you still have faith in the God who calls you to complete devotion? Will you pass the test of faith? When anxiety rises up in your heart and the enemy tells you that you will never get married, will you fight the fight of faith and submit those desires back to the Lord.

Anxiety comes out in many different ways. It often shows its face through our thoughts and words. Again, I'm not using the word anxiety to reference the brain disorder that should be properly treated by medical professionals. The kind of anxiety I am speaking of is the spiritual brokenness of overly caring and worrying about our personal concerns (see 1 Peter 5:7 NASB). For example, I've met so many men and women who live in despair about not being in a relationship that is leading to marriage. As God takes His time to provide our spouses, we become discouraged in our waiting.

Hannah was a woman who waited in despair—and she seemingly had good reason to be angry and upset. She walked around sad because her husband's other wife gave birth to his children continually but the Lord had closed her womb. Hannah would weep day and night to the Lord. Her husband loved her deeply but Hannah's despair could not return the love back to him. Hannah was greatly distressed, prayed to the Lord and wept bitterly (see 1 Sa 1:10 NASB). Listen to how sad her heart is:

> *She made a vow and said, "O Lord of hosts, if You will indeed look on the affliction of Your maidservant and remember me, and not forget Your maidservant, but will give Your maidservant a son, then I will give him to the*

> Lord all the days of his life, and a razor shall never come on his head" (1 Sa 1:11. NASB).

What does your despair and sadness regarding your marital status lead you to? When my heart was sick with the desire to be loved by a man, it led me to many doors I should never have entered. The word *despair* in Greek is Ἐξαπορέομαι, which means to be in extreme despair, implying both anxiety and fear—'to be in utter despair, to despair completely.'[14]

I had a friend that I was extremely close to and for whom I started having feelings. When I say feelings, I mean the worst kind possible for this friend. I started liking him. It happened all of a sudden and I have no idea why, to be honest. We worked closely together and spent a lot of time together. We worked so closely together, his sister asked us both why we weren't interested in each other. I'd learned from previous experience that every desire isn't from the Lord so it was an all out war inside of me to not like this guy. I had dreams of marrying him and the whole nine yards. Once again, my mind was playing tricks on me. I was in despair. I fasted, prayed, confessed, journaled, and did anything other Christian discipline I could think of. My heart was sick. But it was in this instance that I decided to war for my singleness. I experienced what it meant to be at the end of my rope quite like Hannah.

The problem with how I handled all these emotions is that I entertained them. He wasn't pursuing me. A few months later he revealed he was interested in pursuing someone else and in an effort to get over being heartsick (as opposed to bringing them before the Lord), I co-signed his desire and even lent them my car to go out. I had been waiting for 5 years at this point and like Hannah, I was heartsick.

I am not alone. I am sure many of you have experienced being heartsick whether from a love lost, a love not reciprocated, or a love imagined.

Tasha from the *Single and Anxious* web series is an incredible example of a woman thirsty for attention. In season one, we see her chase after Sebastian with a thirst that clearly no man can quench. Sebastian made it incredibly evident that he was not interested in Tasha. He even went as far as to show his affection for her cousin right in front of her. However, that did not stop Tasha from announcing her adoration for Sebastian in every encounter they had with each other. Tasha had yet to learn the value of waiting in her singleness. As the creator of her character, I knew that I wanted a big part of Tasha's thirsty pursuit to reflect her being so desperate to be in a relationship that she would be willing to settle for whoever was available—in this case, Sebastian. Tasha did not know what it felt like to be worth the wait.

In the midst of all our waiting, we experience a deep emptiness that we need the Lord to heal. Waiting exposes us to ourselves. Hannah's waiting not only exposed that her heart was sick about her husband's other wife producing and she being unable to do so. It exposed that she coveted that fact which can easily happen when we despair and lack trust. We covet that which isn't ours. At weddings, we see people in the midst of one of the greatest celebration of their lives. But during this time, there are others who are sitting in the pews watching the ceremony or dancing at the reception, and coveting that experience, allowing jealousy to rise in our hearts. We see the love these couples express toward each other and we covet it. We hate with smiles on our faces because our hearts are sick. We need the hope of God to reign in our hearts and breath life in us while we are waiting.

As a wedding filmmaker, I've shot countless weddings while I was single and it was certainly hard sometimes. I had to put my heart into subjection to the Lord and His plan. At weddings, love is clearly in the air. It is during these times that I learned how to celebrate others and not simply think about my own desires of marriage.

It certainly didn't help that I was often shooting weddings with the man that was courting me—my future husband. Weddings can expose so much about us to us. They can easily cause the lust in our hearts to rise to the surface. The fact that all of the wickedness rises, isn't really the issue though. The heart question is this: Do we surrender our sickness to the Lord while we wait?

Hannah took the affliction of her waiting and turned it over to the Lord. After waiting for years, she knew that the first child she bore was to be given to the Lord. Hannah realized that God had a plan for her child that far exceeded her expectations of being a mother. Once Samuel was weaned from her milk, she gave him to Eli to be raised as a prophet. Hannah turned her sick heart into a healed heart. God could now trust Hannah with his gift because she was willing to give it back to Him.

Abraham's wait was much like Hannah's in that he was tested. When the Lord provides your spouse will you worship Him or will you turn your spouse into an idol? When my husband and I first started courting we realized how easy it was to get wrapped up in one another and not put the Lord in the forefront of our relationship. We absolutely love talking, hanging, creating and simply being with each other. But there was a fine line between loving someone and worshipping them. Worship puts that person, place or thing before God. We had seen couples turn each other into idols and slowly fall away from God and we didn't want that to be our story. For us, a part of addressing our brokenness was addressing the fact that we were prone to make idols out of relationships we'd longed for.

Allowing the Lord to deliver us in our brokenness is worth it. He is not a God who looks at our mess with hate. He looks at our mess with compassion and wants to form us. He's a good Father that desires for us to be what we were designed to be. He wants us to have a testimony like Abraham and Sarah that resonates for generations. A testimony that recounts how we waited patiently and saw the goodness of the Lord fulfilled in the earth. When the Lord cleans out a heart, He is looking to get the glory from it. Remember my issue with pride and vulnerability? Because I was willing to go through that process, He is now able to get the glory from it and others are able to use my experience as a compass for freedom. It profits the Lord nothing for us to simply put rings on our fingers and later divorce because of irreconcilable differences. However, when we wait patiently and deal with our broken hearts, He gets the glory. The more we see the Lord fill the holes in our hearts with His Word, the greater our trust in Him becomes. When we repeatedly see the Lord work, we realize more and more we can trust Him.

A marriage of love, unity, and understanding is not rooted in romance; it is rooted in worship[15]. The opposite of worship of God is idolatry and unfortunately that is what many marriages and children become. There was recently an article going around about parents and children. The article discussed parents putting their children before their spouses. I reposted the article and it became an all out war in my comments section. One wife and mother of two defended her children being first before her marriage. She went on to argue that her husband was an adult and could take care of himself. I then went on to remind her in a loving way that her covenant before God was with her husband not her children. Her children most certainly mattered but they were to be loved not worshipped. "Idolatry may not involve explicit denials of God's existence or character. It may well come in the form of an over-attachment to something that is, in itself, perfectly good... An idol can be a physical object, a property, a person, an activity, a role, an institution, a hope, an image, an idea, a pleasure, a hero—anything that can substitute for God."[16] Marriage and family will not fill the deep well of loneliness that exists in your heart. Marriage will only expose the well even more.

I made a lot of mistakes in my singleness but learning that contentment is found only in Jesus made the rest of my waiting well worth it. The goal of our lives is not to be healed from broken, sick hearts so that we can have better marriages but to be healed so that we can be better children to our loving God. Jesus must be our obsession. When we discover that other things—including relationships—are clouding our hearts from being fully devoted to the Lord, we must address them. No matter what you encounter in your wait, Jesus is enough. You may have made mistakes similar to Gina and

Mark, or me, Abraham or Hannah, but we see in the midst of all these stories that God can restore any broken heart and teach it to trust Him. Let your wait give Him glory and be counted as righteousness in the books of your legacy.

> *Without becoming weak in faith he contemplated his own body, now as good as dead since he was about a hundred years old, and the deadness of Sarah's womb; yet, with respect to the promise of God, he did not waver in unbelief but grew strong in faith, giving glory to God, and being fully assured that what God had promised, He was able also to perform. Therefore it was also credited to him as righteousness* (Rom 4:19-22 NASB).

AN EXERCISE IN REFLECTION

Write the answer to the following questions: If I <u>never</u> get married, will I still have faith in the God who calls me to complete devotion? List what might be stopping you from devoting your singleness completely to God.

_____
_____
_____
_____
_____
_____

After you have made your list, say out loud after each one of them the following sentences:
- God loves me just the way I am.
- Marriage doesn't complete me. I'm already complete.
- I am loved by God.
- Singleness is not a disease.

A Prayer

Jesus, this was a really hard chapter for me. Waiting isn't easy and I haven't always done a good job of it. I need you right now to show me where I can lean on You in my waiting. Help me not to settle and move ahead of you while I long to be loved by a spouse. Love is worth waiting for so help me work on being loved by you while I wait on a mate that is right for me. Jesus, if I never marry, give me the courage to be content with just that. Remind me that not having a mate doesn't make me less than but it gives me more time to give you my undivided attention while you work on me. In Jesus' Name, Amen.

Chapter Four

Eye Candy: How to Live Pure

Me on Facebook: *Rode past a fly dude. My flesh wants to look more, but my Spirit keeps me focused and says nahhh, no entrance for the enemy!*

Comment by friend on Facebook: *Is it that serious, Chris? Try thanking God for the eye candy and for the wisdom He gave you to know that's all it can be for now. Sheesh!*

The response of my friend on social media didn't surprise me but it did make me think. She asked if it really was that deep and at first I thought, "Girl, you have no idea!" However, at the time, I could not articulate why it was so important not to look. Living a pure life is challenging. Your ability to remain firm increases while your tolerance decreases. I thought and pondered my friends comment more and then began to think about what "eye candy" really means. While at a Bible study that same night, someone mentioned something about candy and my friend's words popped back in my mind. Too much candy can make your teeth rot. For me, a little bit of candy can entice my desire for more sugar and that increase in sugar has the ability to spoil my appetite. In this case, spoil my appetite for the Lord and stop me from enjoying the incredible joys of my husband. In that moment, I realized I didn't want candy. I wanted a nutritious meal that only the Lord could give me through my husband. As the years have gone on, I have realized the difference between looking in lust and looking to admire the beauty of a human being. I workout a lot and I love to look at fitness magazines and Instagram accounts. But, again, there is a distinct difference between looking in admiration or to understand how a muscle works and looking for lustful pleasure. That day, driving down the street, my mind wasn't on beauty. It was on sex, and I had to avoid that at all cost. That candy was not my husband.

This world has no desire to promote anything nutritious. After all, it is greed and lust that keeps the economy thriving. Eye candy is everywhere! Turn on the television—eye candy. Walk down the street—eye candy. Watch your favorite show and it's like a porn flick in the middle of an incredible story or production. Even turn on Nickelodeon and there is a 13-year-old little boy giving your children a desire for eye candy. It is everywhere. And we all know that candy tastes good in the beginning. Think about it! Sex is incredible, masturbation feels good, and porn is available whenever you want it. Sex is so incredible that Google, in about 0.73 seconds, gives you about 3,030,000,000 results by typing in the three-letter word.

Most parents encourage their children to have sex. Sure, they normally tell them to wait until they are "grown" and in a mature relationship. Very few parents today encourage their children to wait until marriage. Why wait until marriage? Shouldn't you test the product? This is the general consensus on the topic of sex before marriage.

But this is not God's way.

Holy Kisses and Pillows

My mother never knew what to think of me. One moment she was giving me a box of condoms at the age of 16 and telling me to make sure to use them. The next, she was asking me to let her know if I wanted birth control. A few months after that, she might be saying that it was OK if I was gay and that she'd still love me. So no wonder I had no idea what purity was when I got saved. As mentioned earlier, in 2004, I just decided not to give any parts of my body away anymore—even within my virginity. I was exhausted and tired of feeling guilty for putting my mouth on penis' that weren't mine by marriage. Purity is high on God's agenda.[17] Often, people think that they cannot live without sex. "God created me with this desire," they say. "Wasn't the body created to have sex? That's why it feels so good." Of course sex was created by God and yes, He created it to feel good. However, it was never in God's plan for people to have sex outside of marriage.

People have sex outside of marriage because they are anxious. How do I know? I've been there. I was anxious to be loved, anxious to be wanted, and anxious to be held. I wanted to get as much candy out of the candy machine without paying the price of commitment. Any commitment outside of marriage is not a commitment at all; it is a test drive.

"Let me see if this is what I want before I buy it."

"I like it, but I don't like it enough to keep it."

Our desire for the benefits of marriage, drive us into sexual and emotional immorality. These desires show us where our affections are. When God is the lover of your soul and holds all your affections, you learn that through His grace and power you can resist the desires of your being.

Please understand you can't do it on your own. Sexual purity should be a result of your desire to honor God with your body. It doesn't just happen. The kingdom mindset concerning sex and emotional purity must be cultivated. It is a consistent process of weeding out the old thought patterns and saturating the pruned space with the Word of God.

The lack of sexual purity in ones life is a clear indication of a prideful heart that refuses to seek and trust God for His Kingdom agenda as it pertains to him or her. We exalt our own desires above God's desires for us. Purity is not just a matter of abstaining from sexual and intimate relationships. There are individuals who have never been in relationships and even those who are abstaining from sex, who are still not living with God's renewed mind. My desire is that each of us would walk with minds that are renewed toward singleness, sex, and purity in intimacy. Paul gives a great illustration of what a renewed mind looks like:

> *"But you did not learn Christ in this way, if indeed you have heard Him and have been taught in Him, just as truth is in Jesus, that, in reference to your former manner of life, you lay aside the old self, which is being corrupted in accordance with the lusts of deceit, and that you be renewed in the spirit of your mind, and put on the new self, which in the likeness of God has been create."* (Eph. 4:20-24 NASB)

Scripture says, "God has chosen the foolish things of[18] the world to shame."[19] The fact that you have read this far means you desire to honor God in your singleness. But be clear: that also means purity in intimacy. It will not be easy. However, it will be rewarding and the daily fight will lessen the more you engage God through prayer, His Word, and transparent fellowship with other mature believers.

You have been brought with a price and given the gift of salvation through Jesus Christ (see Ephesians 2:8, Romans 6:23). Included in the sale is your ability to use the spiritual discipline of the faith to overcome any issues you have with emotional and sexual purity. The power of Christ has made that available to you. What will you do with the gift? Will you treat it like a piece of candy? Suck all the sugar out and when there is nothing left, discard it along with the candy wrapper?

Have you ever chewed gum? Of course you have. Often I chew gum to keep me focused. I put the gum in my mouth and it gives me this incredible burst of flavor. Like, *wow, that tastes good!* But then I discover that, after only a good 30 minutes of chewing, there is no more flavor in the gum. I have used the gum beyond its ability. The gum was not designed to last a lifetime. It was designed to give you a little something and then make you move on to the next piece of gum.

And that's exactly how we treat sex and our bodies.

In college, my girls and I would always chill together. It never failed when we got together that the subjects of love, sex, and relationships would come up. We talked about sex more than anything. One thing that was the common denominator amongst us all was that our fathers weren't in the home. All of us rejected commitment and we loved to talk about sex. Entering college, I didn't have much sexual experience. I had experimented in elementary school, been molested in my childhood and adolescent years and, as I noted before, was afraid of anything that looked like commitment while in high school. I would mess around with guys but I never got into a real committed relationship. Ironically, my resistance to commitment is what kept me from going all the way in college. I didn't want to give my body completely away without a commitment. I didn't mind them eating some of my candy but they couldn't have all of it.

That sounded reasonable while I was in college--until I got saved and discovered that giving a dude *any* of my candy was against God's will. My eyes too often deceived me. I liked what I saw so I went after every dude I desired whether he knew he wanted me or not. My aim was to make him want me. Sometimes I got him, other times I didn't. I remember one evening my girls and I were drinking and one of our male friends came through with his homies from New York. We all partnered up with dudes we didn't know. My two friends took the beds so my guy and I went into the student lounge and attacked each other like straight animals. Exchanging oral sex and kissing so hard I ended up with about 6 hickeys. I didn't even know him! Like, I didn't know his name. What was even crazier was the next day I was hosting a concert with Joe Buddens and my main dude was coming up to hang with us. When I discovered the hickeys the next morning, my homegirl came over with a wooden brush to try and get rid of them. Not only was I embarrassed that it had even happened but they went absolutely nowhere. I ended up wearing a short-sleeved turtleneck on an extremely hot summer day.

Sugar Cleanse

The culture has infected us with an extreme desire for eye candy. We laugh at 2 and 3 year olds when they dance to Beyoncé's hit song, *Single Ladies*. It's cute to us. But the song deposits seeds of rebellion against God and our bodies. Imagine your little cousin coming up to you and saying, "*Cuz if you liked it then you should have put a ring on it. If you liked it then you shoulda put a ring on it. Don't be mad once you see that he want it.*" Most of us don't even pay attention to the lyrics of the song, but it reflects the world's logic that says, "If you like my body. Then you will want to marry me." This song is essentially teaching your little cousin that she should have sex with another man because the one she was in a relationship with didn't desire to marry her. Now don't get me wrong—Bey is an incredible artist. However, the song promotes one thing: that he had *it* already and before *it* left he should've put a ring on it

Or take Trey Songz, for example. He is so confident in his unmarried sexual abilities that he proclaims in a song that he *Invented Sex*. Are you so cocky about your sexual ability that you spit your venomous words of enticement into the ears of your next conquest? I know I used to. That's how I hooked and pulled them. Just because you aren't having penetration doesn't mean you're staying pure. I was an impure fellatio giving and receiving jawn. Just tell them how good you are in bed and that lust will pull them right in. Everyone seems to be looking for a little sexual pleasure. *Tinder* is full of men and women looking to hook up. Yes, it feels good but it also cuts you off from the God of love and grace that desires to show you a love that is more pleasurable and desirable than what you think you can accomplish with your body.

I'm not going to front on you like eye candy doesn't look good. It looks incredible and tastes delicious. When we give eye candy any of our time, we come in agreement with satan against God's plan for our lives. Don't believe me? Let's take a walk through human beings first encounter with sin.

The set up: God created this incredible earth. He created Adam and then decided to give him a wife. God gives Adam specific instructions about not eating the forbidden fruit. Adam relays that information to Eve. Genesis 3 states, *"When the woman saw that the tree was good for food, and that it was a delight to the eyes, and that the tree was desirable to make one wise, she took from its fruit and ate; and she gave also to her husband with her, and he ate"* (Gen. 3:6 NASB). Eve's deception was in the eye candy. She "saw" that it was good. We think that sex is good because we first see the physical possibilities in the potential partner.

The fruit was a "delight to her eyes." Eve thought that God was holding back on her. Satan whispered sweet nothings of deception in her ear. So much so that she was able to convince Adam to eat the fruit as well. "For God to single this out from the beginning means we must understand desire. In addition to what I have pointed out above, we need to understand that desire is linked to the heart and eyes."[20]

Every kingdom has ethics. Are you willing to submit yourself to the sexual and emotional ethics of God's kingdom so that His glory can shine through you? Purity is not designed for you to be a nun. It is designed for you to fall madly in love with the only one that can love you the way your heart yearns and aches for on a daily basis—God.

AN EXERCISE IN REFLECTION

You have been brought with a price. Included in the sale is your ability to use the spiritual discipline of the faith to overcome your lack of emotional and sexual purity. The power of Christ has made that available to you. Ponder the following questions:

- Are you fighting for Christ to be your only devotion?
- Do you want to be sexually pure?
- Is purity good news to you?
- Are you willing to guard your heart and body to remain pure?
- Does sexual purity scare you? Why or why not?

Prayer Bursts

Lord, help me to honor and appreciate my body and the freedom you gave me.

Jesus, purity begins in my mind and heart so please give me the desire to please you with the whole of me.

Jesus, help me lean on your Word and let it heal me from the inside out.

Give me strength for when I am weak and when I condemn myself. Where sin is shown in my life, help me to see that there is more grace for me to receive.

Jesus, when my emotions and desires attempt to seduce me with temporary pleasures, remind me of your goodness and your present help. In Jesus' name, amen.

Chapter Five

The Promise of Your Singleness

You might have noticed that it is the halfway point of the book and I haven't spoken much about marriage, relationships, and courtship outside of the realm of our hearts needing to be mended and the developing of our ability to wait and remain pure in our singleness. A part of that has to do with my own wrestlings with the subject. I am now writing this book as a married woman and I see things from both sides of the track, if you will. I absolutely love my single brothers and sisters and I see their desire to be married. I also see their desire to find fulfillment without a mate as well. So many of the books I read as a single were geared toward emphasizing the importance of keeping my legs closed but very few dealt with *why* my legs were open or why, for the brothers, their sausage was inside of hot pockets. Too many of us have been born and bred in unhealthy homes and spent far too much time around friends who had the same upbringing.

Sitting on my friend's bed in college, I finally realized we had a major problem! As I said, all we ever talked about was sex, guys, drinking and schoolwork (sometimes). We were bad influences on each other but that's all we knew. We were attention hungry young ladies who were yearning for true love or whatever we thought that meant. Most of the time we simply settled for a few calls and text messages to arrange jump offs (sexual contact with no strings). We weren't giving each other life with our words but instead we were exposing each other to more darkness. Being single and sexually free became a way of life.

While writing the outline for this book and the corresponding web series, I decided to take a new approach. How do I encourage singles to seek the Lord more than their wants? I didn't want to write another relationship book filled with how to remain pure until your mate comes or how to not have sex. Those types of books certainly have their place but there are too many of them. As a single, I wanted to hear about cleaning out my heart and desiring Jesus more than my desire for a mate. I needed to come to a point where marriage didn't matter. It wasn't until I came to the revelation that Jesus is truly enough that I found peace in my heart.

When Jesus is enough, there is a level of freedom that works from the inside out. Instead of focusing on not being in a relationship, our focus should be on what keeps us out of a good relationship with Jesus. If you have baggage while not in a relationship, you will certainly have baggage in the relationship. And the truth about baggage is that only Jesus can remove it from our hearts. No amount of love can remove baggage from your heart if it's not the love of God.

Have you ever truly asked the Lord about the purpose of your singleness? Sexual purity should be a result of your desire to honor God with your body. Anyone can be celibate. There are certainly unsaved virgins. So besides being celibate, what is the purpose of your singleness? What has God specifically crafted this time for? Do you really think He has given you the gift of singleness so that you can hang out with your friends, travel, and go to Christian events? Has He given you the gift of singleness so that you can spend your daily thoughts hoping to be in a relationship? Or, here is radical question: Has God given you the gift of singleness to empty out your life in devotion and service to others? Scripture implies the latter. Being single is a gift. It's not a spiritual gift. It is a gift of time. It's a gift that you can use and use until it's gone. Once you are no longer single, the ability to use your time as you freely wish will be gone.

The Gift of Time

As a now married woman I truly do understand the gift of time. One of the greatest things I miss about being single is sleeping over my girlfriends' houses and vice versa. I don't think I ever realized how much I hung out with my homies. It was nothing to stay over one of their houses. It was common for one of us to say, "Hey, I want to watch a movie tonight, your house or mine?" Nowadays, I don't even think about sleepovers. I'm home every night with my husband and vice-versa because my attention is called to him. With my career, I am able to have sleepovers while on business trips with my girls because we work together but it's still not the same. As a single, you may have time commitments but there aren't any commitments that are consistently attached to a spouse.

In 1st Corinthians, we discover God's desire for singles. In an attempt to explain the importance of sexual relations only in the confines of marriage, Paul expresses the responsibilities of a married person and a single person (see 1 Cor. 7:1–2 NASB)

> *The husband must fulfill his duty to his wife, and likewise also the wife to her husband. The wife does not have authority over her own body, but the husband does; and likewise also the husband does not have authority over his own body, but the wife does.* (1 Co 7:3-4 NASB)

Husbands and wives have duties to one another. A duty as described here, isn't drudgery but a responsibility to serve and love another; to put your spouse before all others besides the Lord. A single is not bound by a covenant, or this kind of duty. Instead, as a single, you have a duty to the Lord. The single person's duty is to give the Lord devoted attention.

> *But I want you to be free from concern. One who is unmarried is concerned about the things of the Lord, how he may please the Lord; but one who is married is concerned about the things of the world, how he may please his wife, and his interests are divided. The woman who is unmarried, and the virgin, is concerned about the things of the Lord, that she may be holy both in body and spirit; but one who is married is concerned about the things of the world, how she may please her husband. This I say for your own benefit; not to put a restraint upon you, but to promote what is appropriate and to secure undistracted devotion to the Lord.*[21]

One of the reasons singleness is so challenging is that we are too often concerned with the wrong things. God didn't provide the gift of singleness for you to be concerned with getting married. He created the gift of singleness so that you would not have to be concerned. That's not easy but it's certainly possible. It is possible to be so devoted to the Lord that marriage is not a concern for you.

When I first started my fight for purity as a single, it seemed impossible! When a guy walked in the room and was a cutie, I imagined he was my husband. I attached my first name to his last. I didn't have to know anything about his character, calling, or purpose. My thoughts were contaminated by my past. It became evident that closing my legs and overcoming lust was not as challenging as rebuilding my heart for God. Fornication was no longer an option in my heart. However, emotional instability was. I felt the immediate conviction of the Holy Spirit when I had lustful thoughts, however, I was less prone to acknowledge that same conviction regarding my emotions.

Emotions have a way of justifying themselves to the point where we end up believing the lies they can tell. Are you believing the lie that your singleness is a disease? I understand singleness is scary. Society has gone from folks getting married at 18 to online dating sites to our barely wanting to get married—all in the span of a couple of generations. We are the first generation where marriage after 30 is the standard. But deep down, all of us want to be loved. I know I did. The main reason I stepped back from dating was that I didn't know who I was outside of chasing guys and being chased. Is that you? If so, I get it. Commercially, we are told we need to be in a relationship. If you watch television, use popular Christian dating sites, they all will tell you how to find companionship. There are apps, Facebook and Instagram feeds, with pictures and memes telling you that you aren't complete without a relationship. However, God's Word tells us that we are complete as singles and that our devotion should be to the Lord.

The Antidote

Singleness isn't a disease, it's a cure. It is a time of freedom. Freedom to live and learn. The cure singleness provides is found in wrestling with your anxieties, frustrations, and heartbreaks. It is found in spending countless minutes of the day speaking to the Lord in your head, on your knees, or in a journal. Your singleness doesn't need to be fixed. You are perfect with or without a mate. I know it is shocking to hear from a married woman, but I believe singles need to consistently hear it. I loved being single. I eventually learned to be content. I learned to not allow my anxiety to overtake me. And let me tell you a secret most married people are afraid to admit: Marriage doesn't remove insecurity, loneliness, habits, lust, brokenness, trust issues, or anything else. Instead, it exposes those things all the more to sanctify you.

The purpose of our devotion to God is to be faithful to the Lord. The word *devotion* in 1st Corinthians 7 is *euparedros*. It means to be steadfast, faithful.[22] So often we desire to be faithful and devoted to another person instead of the Lord. The Lord will fulfill you and be your everything. He is the only One who can take away the loneliness in our hearts. It is imaginary thinking if you assume that a relationship or marriage will cure your loneliness. Instead, you will be just as lonely in a relationship or marriage as you were without it. Devotion to the Lord means being steadfast regardless of the distractions. You can't be steadfast for the Lord if your emotions are far away from Him. How do I know? I lived that life. When I first accepted the Lord I was dating a lot of dudes at once. My emotions were all over the place. I would read my Bible in the morning and journal but it was all about the guy I really wanted to date. Remember the light-skinned rapper? Well, the relationship with him is what drove me to journaling. I wasn't asking the Lord to work on my heart. I was journaling my frustrations and then acting them out in *Can you come over?* phone calls and text messages. I was taking steps toward the Lord but my focus was on him. I wasn't going hard for Jesus. I was going hard to get to this guy; because he mattered more to me than Jesus at the time.

Being single and anxious focuses our attention on our desires and not our faithfulness to the Lord. What pleases the Lord is a single person being devoted solely to Him in duty. He is your focus. He is your Comforter. He is your best friend. He is your everything. He is who you call when you are going through trouble at work. If God isn't all of these things, most likely there are idols in your heart that are preventing you from being devoted to Him. When you are devoted to the Lord you are constantly in service. God can send you to another country, change your vacation plans, or even lead you into all night prayer. Being constantly in service to God is a gift from the Lord. The gift of singleness is undistracted devotion to the Lord[23]. How sweet it is to be able to allow your life to be organized and planned by Him.

In our culture, it is unheard of to be undistracted especially in devotion to God. When some think of devotion, they don't immediately think of Jesus. Some think of a wife who does all that she can to make sure the needs of her husband and family are taken care of. Some may also think of a single parent taking care of their children and working two to three jobs to make ends meet. Can you think of any single people who are devoted to the Lord? Who popped in your mind? What about that person is inspiring? What can you glean from them? That's the type of single person you should long to be.

Being devoted to the Lord doesn't mean you become a nun and take a lifetime vow to serve Him and give up your right of marriage. Being devoted to the Lord means becoming committed to His will for your life whether it is to be married or not. Can I let you in on a little secret? Everyone will not be married. No matter how great your desire for marriage is, it is not a guarantee of life.

Recently, I had the opportunity to send some quality time with a woman who is in her fifties and single. She spoke of her desire to be married and have children but after years of waiting she finally surrendered those desires to the Lord. I can't say that this is a happily ever after story where she ended getting married later in life. No, she found peace with the will of God. Now that woman spends her time devoted to the Lord and appreciative that the Lord is with her and for her. Singleness is a time to maximize your devotion to the Lord. If you have been living a life of frustration because you're still single, take some time now to repent and talk to the Lord regarding your heart. Devotion to the Lord is joyous. It should not be done out of religious duty but out of a heart flowing with love knowing that you are your Beloved's and your Beloved is yours.

Count the Cost of Love

> *But if you marry, you have not sinned; and if a virgin marries, she has not sinned. Yet such will have trouble in this life, and I am trying to spare you. But this I say, brethren, the time has been shortened, so that from now on those who have wives should be as though they had none; and those who weep, as though they did not weep; and those who rejoice, as though they did not rejoice; and those*

> *who buy, as though they did not possess; and those who use the world, as though they did not make full use of it; for the form of this world is passing away. But I want you to be free from concern. One who is unmarried is concerned about the things of the Lord, how he may please the Lord.* (1 Co 7:28-32 NASB)

Marriage isn't a sin as Paul explains here, but it does add a new level of difficulty to your life. In no way does this verse suggest you be celibate for life, but it does suggest that you count the costs. To be free from concern is to have only one thing to focus on. A single person's focus should be focused on the things of the Lord. If the Lord isn't making a way for your courtship to begin, then it isn't a concern. Singleness provides freedom and makes way for God's agenda. It allows the time to pass without distraction. If your heart is divided, you aren't serving the Lord.

Anxiety doesn't easily go away but it can be churned out of your well. The well of your heart is full of concerns and the Lord desires to give you a pure well. The well of our hearts is a deep place. It's where all our emotions live. When you have a pure well, you can drop your bucket and drink from it immediately. However, if your well isn't pure, you have to add chlorine to the water and rinse the well of all its impurities.

For about a year and half, I had the opportunity to live on a property that was supplied by well water. When I first visited this missionary campus, they didn't have any bottled water. I asked if there was a Brita, water cooler, something I could get drinking water from because I was thirsty. The store wasn't in walking distance and living in Philly for so long, I never drank straight faucet water. The missionaries looked at me crazy. He immediately told me that they had faucet water. I was extremely thirsty, so I had no choice. With one sip of the tap water, I knew something was different. I'd never tasted anything like it. It was perfect drinking water. I asked what kind of water it was because it surely didn't come from the regular tap water in state of Pennsylvania and he immediately replied, "Oh it's well water." Well water is amazing.

Within a few months, I received an email asking that I do not drinking the water for a day because they would be washing the well with chlorine in order to clean all the junk out of the well. That's when it dawned on me. God uses His Word just like that—to clean our emotional wells. As you continue to go through your journey and fight the anxiety of your singleness, cleaning your well will be of more importance than just getting married.

Our minds need to be renewed about the purpose of our singleness. Many of us waste valuable years doing nothing when God is calling us to a higher place of devotion to Him. When you consider what it means to be devoted, think about the experience of getting to know someone. When we meet a new person we click with, we want to know everything about them. We want to spend time with them. We begin to contact each other about meeting at certain places and hanging out more. This reminds me of the time right after college when I met a really close friend of mine. This sister and I just clicked! We lived in different states but we figured out how to grow our sisterhood. We both understood the purpose of our singleness and we wanted to grow in God. Through fellowship, we supported each other and valued what the Lord was doing in our lives. We were faithful friends. That is exactly what devotion to the Lord looks like. Devotion is spending time with the Lord through prayer, fellowship, the Word, serving and being intentional about loving on Jesus, and letting Him love on you.

Devotion takes daily commitment. When you are committed to a person, place, or thing, you put their desires and needs before your own. As you are being formed into the image of God, you will become more like Him and discover what He desires for you in your singleness. You begin to learn that God has a purpose for you as a single and it is being completely satisfied in Him. Being *single and satisfied* isn't a cliché. It isn't a saying on a t-shirt you wear to avoid questions about why you're single. Being single and satisfied is about

Jesus being enough for eternity whether you are married or not.

What the apostle Paul advised us to do is to live life by eternal values because our time here on earth is short. Since marriage is one of those things that will pass away, Paul didn't want us to fix our whole lives on it. God has a purpose for singleness. If you are single and spending all of your time wanting to be married, then you are missing God's purpose for you. And that means you are not getting all that God has for you in the time He's given you.[24]

God has given us time to come closer to Him. If you ask anyone who received salvation after they were married, they will tell you that it is hard to devote time to the Lord. It's not that it is impossible but but being able to develop a deep, loving relationship with Jesus without certain responsibilities is a gift.

There's a stranger in my bed

Waking up at 4am, I often sit on my bed crying out to the Lord to fix my heart and give me a heart for people. As a married woman, I have to get up and leave the room when this happens in order not to wake my husband. In marriage, even my devotional life had to shift. But I'd learned how to deal with that much earlier in life. She wasn't my spouse but there was someone else who shared a room with me long before my husband did.

It came as a surprise to me when I first felt the Lord impress upon my heart that I should invite an 18 year old to live with my roommate, Olivia, and me. On one of our regular trips to Trader Joe's, a few sisters and I ran into this young lady who I will call Mariah. She was a girl known by another young woman I knew. I was instantly drawn to her. Mariah was one of the most beautiful girls I'd ever seen but I could also see deep pain in her heart. We all prayed for Mariah in the car that night and went on about our lives.

A few weeks later, while doing my seminary residency at Children's Hospital, I was roaming the halls checking on patients when I stumbled into Mariah's room. I had no idea she was in the hospital but I took it as a sign from God. When I walked in that room I didn't know that my life would forever be changed by a teenager in need. It turned out that Mariah was about to be homeless and no longer welcome in her mother's home. Immediately my heart felt for her and I took her home.

Here's the thing: when I decided to allow an unemployed 18 year old with no current vision of her future to live in my apartment along with my roommate, my whole life changed. I had no idea the emotional and spiritual muscles I would need to develop all because I brought Mariah into our lives. One of the biggest transitions that took place in my life was not having the ability to freely worship, read, and pray aloud.

Why?

Because we not only shared a room, we shared a bed.

See, I wasn't aware of how much time I spent with the Lord undistracted until I no longer could do that in my bed without waking her up. I could no longer just wake up and cry aloud to the Lord without waking her. I got a small taste of what it would feel like to have my attention divided.

And Mariah definitely took a lot of my time. I became like a mother to her and had concern for her spiritual, physical, and emotional needs. While this wasn't exactly a reflection of marriage, I learned the importance of being aware of someone in your personal space. Prior to this experience, I knew the purpose of my singleness but I didn't grasp the value of my *time* as a single person. Through having Mariah in my life, the Lord gave me a full on example of what it would mean to share my room with another person and be concerned for their well being physically, spiritually and emotionally. I didn't realize the value of my time before Mariah. I didn't appreciate my time until it was gone.

Are you allowing the Lord to wake you in the middle of the night to cry out to Him? If you share a room, are you going into the bathroom or waiting to have those undistracted times with the Lord? Familiarity will breed a lack of value if you aren't intentional about your life with the Lord. What do you have in your toolbox that you aren't using?

When you are free from concern, you aren't anxious. It doesn't make sense to me when people move in with each other before they get married. Even when I wasn't a believer, it didn't. Why buy the almonds to make almond milk when the carton milk is already made and ready for you? The idea behind moving in is to try it and see if you want to buy it. No woman who is currently living free from anxiety would *ever* try this. When a woman moves in with a man, what she is saying is, "I would like to marry you." What a man is often saying is, "I'm not sure if I want to marry you. Let's save some money and see how this works." That is a recipe for concern.

Free from concern means free from "anxious" concern (*amerimnos*, without anxiety) about *the affairs of this world* or family matters (not to be confused with "worldliness" as that term has come to be understood).[25]

Are you sitting in the bleachers being a spectator of your destiny because you're concerned about everything? The issue in 1 Corinthians 7 is about time and responsibilities. It isn't about choosing to be a nun but it's about how will you use the time that you have given and will you dive wholeheartedly into the plan and purpose of your singleness? This is not to place restrictions on you. I want you to do whatever will help you serve the Lord best, with as few distractions as possible (see 1 Cor. 7:35 NASB). What distractions exist in your life?

If we are being honest, America is a huge distraction. Our phones are by our bedsides. When we wake up, we check notifications. When we are at work, we are thinking of leaving. As singles, you have to be violent about eliminating these distractions. If the Lord is calling you to be devoted to Him alone, then satan is calling you to be distracted. It is spiritually profitable to make habits that shape your life in God now. Without routine, the pull of nonessential distractions will overpower us. But if we create a routine that enshrines the essentials, we will begin to execute them on autopilot.[26]

When I was new in the Lord, I kept hearing messages about the importance of quiet time. Note: quiet time can occur at any time of the day. Throughout my years as a believer, I have realized that spending time with the Lord early in the morning, before my day gets started, are the most important moments of my day. When we spend time with the Lord in the morning, He is able to clean, purge, and order our steps for the day. The more time you spend with the Lord, the more you are sensitive to His presence. The problem for many of us is learning how to quiet our minds in order to focus on the Lord and not all the thoughts floating around in our heads.

Instead of going into prayer with a mountain of thoughts and things to do on your mind, write them down on a piece of paper and keep that piece of paper by your side as you pray. It will help you tremendously to simply dump the thought somewhere else.

Another stumbling block of prioritizing time with the Lord is not knowing *what* to pray. How many times has someone asked you to pray for them and you forgot? I have practiced creating prayer calendars where I cover specific people, needs, and wants everyday as to not lose track. When you are forming the habit of devoted time with the Lord, be flexible and allow the Holy Spirit to move you. God doesn't move the same in every season of life. As the actual seasons change, so does how God wants to meet with you. How I met with Him last year isn't the same as how I meet with Him this year. I go through seasons of God waking me up in the middle of the night to speak to me. Those seasons are difficult for some people because of the comfort of their pillows. Can God wake you up in the middle of the night? With me, in the beginning, He couldn't. But the more I prioritized Him, the more I wanted to hear what He had to say to me. When you have a grace filled routine to meet with the Lord on a daily basis, He becomes a priority not a default when things get hard.

The Lord wants to speak to us when we are hurting— and when times are going great. When times are going well we tend to depend on ourselves more because we don't have a sense of our need for Him. We need circumcised hearts for the Lord. This idea of a circumcised heart comes from the Hebrews. The first mention of circumcision was in Genesis 17.

> "This is My covenant, which you shall keep, between Me and you and your descendants after you: every male among you shall be circumcised. And you shall be circumcised in the flesh of your foreskin, and it shall be the sign of the covenant between Me and you. (Gen 17:10-11 NASB)

The covenant was sealed with the circumcision of all the males. Circumcision in our day and time is for health reasons. They remove the skin of the male's penis because it is still believed that it will stay cleaner that way. We do it at birth, but the Israelites performed circumcision as a coming of age, rite of passage for males.

When New Testament believers refer to circumcision, it is for the purpose of our hearts not our bodies. We are not living under the Law so physical circumcision is not an absolute. However, Paul explains in Romans 2 the difference between a person whose heart is circumcised and one whose body is circumcised.

> For indeed circumcision is of value if you practice the Law; but if you are a transgressor of the Law, your circumcision has become uncircumcision. So if the uncircumcised man keeps the requirements of the Law, will not his uncircumcision be regarded as circumcision? And he who is physically uncircumcised, if he keeps the Law, will he not judge you who though having the letter of the Law and circumcision are a transgressor of the Law? For he is not a Jew who is one outwardly, nor is circumcision that which is outward in the flesh. But he is a Jew who is one inwardly; and circumcision is that which is of the heart, by the Spirit, not by the letter; and his

praise is not from men, but from God (Ro 2:25-29 NASB)

Circumcision of the heart is a sign of its position before the Lord. When the Lord is able to cut our hearts and remove what causes infection, we become known as those who are led by the letter and not the law. This kind of circumcision is a way to be identified as God's possession without using external means. It is always a heart issue. When God circumcises your heart, He shows you that He loves you and that your devotion to Him isn't because of your own works but His death and resurrection. Your ability to be completely devoted to God isn't based on how much you read, pray and fellowship. It's based on the actual heart that does all those good Christian disciplines designed to draw us closer to Him. With a circumcised heart, we are inside of the new covenant made possible by the blood of Jesus the Christ. Therefore, being single is less about you and more about God using your life for His glory.

True Satisfaction

When we look at Jesus, we see a single man that sacrificed His all for us. A man on purpose. Instead of being concerned with His right to have a wife on earth, He was devoted to the Father's will for Him to prepare an eternal bride (the church). Just like the Israelites got caught up with the old covenant's need for circumcision (natural), we as believers too often get caught up with our want for spouses and companionship. As you devote your life to the Lord, He will begin to illuminate the eternal promise He has made to you, His bride (spiritual). You are already married and He's coming back for you.

Singleness is a gift to the Lord that requires devotion in order to get all of what you need in this season of your life. Whether you will be married or live a life of singleness, Jesus is enough in both seasons. Marriage is a gift as well but it's no greater than the gift of singleness.

Satisfaction in Jesus is the most important aspect of your singleness. As you build a heart for the Lord remember that Jesus is your priority and that this season may not last forever. If you have a desire to be married, then exhaust your singleness! Spend countless hours with the Lord, serve in your local church, discover your calling, build relationships with other singles on the same road, hang around folks with healthy marriages, travel, have fun, enjoy life, spend more time thinking of things that are lovely and less on what you don't have. With all the distractions in the world, it takes intentionality to make Jesus your devotion. It's not impossible, but it is a fight that you have been equipped to win.

Being single isn't a punishment despite what the world tells you. Your ability to take daily steps in making Jesus your devotion, matter to God. He is honored and glorified by every little step. Even if you have fallen into temptation, His forgiveness is available to bring you back into His arms and restore your relationship with Him. If you are already devoted to the Lord, ask Him to take you deeper into His ocean of grace. We can never exhaust the Lord's heart for us. His heart is greater than the size of any planet and every time you dig into His Word you can discover a new treasure that reignites your faithfulness to Him.

AN EXERCISE IN REFLECTION

Can you think of any single people who are devoted to the Lord? Who popped in your mind? Write down the characteristics he or she has, that you would like to exude yourself.

_____
_____
_____
_____
_____
_____

After you've written this person's qualities, write next to each one of them the following sentences, only finished:
- I am…
- I walk in…
- I will be…
- I will use my singleness to…

A Prayer

Jesus, you are amazing. You don't make any mistakes. During my singleness, help me to appreciate every ounce of time I get to freely share with You. Thank You for giving me the gift of time. Teach me how to be satisfied with where I am instead of worrying about where I am not. Help me to see the tools in my toolbox that I have now to build a life of contentment in you. Give me the courage to live an audacious and fulfilled life as a single in You. In Jesus' name, Amen.

Chapter Six

Building a Heart For God

Growing up, I was always the builder or tech person in the family. From the age of 7, I was putting together VCRs and cable boxes. I had brothers, but they didn't have any skills putting things together. I remembered wondering what they were going to do when I was grown and gone. Instead of learning how to build and put things together, I suppose they'd hire people to do it. In the same way my brothers were dependent on me to build things and put together the tech needs of our home, building a heart for God requires dependency. God isn't interested in our ability to repair our own heart. He wants to be our builder. He is interested in our ability to allow the Holy Spirit to repair our hearts.

In the midst of all the love God gives for our weakness, He is looking for us to receive that love. So many of us have tried to build our own hearts and have failed miserably. God is the fixer, we are not, and that is a hard pill to swallow. All of our lives, we have depended on others and ourselves to build our hearts and lead us to success and love. Our lack of dependency and trust in God is a direct result of our pride — our unwillingness to shift our attention to the Lord. Although we are faithless toward God time and time again, He is not faithless towards us.

> *It is a trustworthy statement; For if we died with Him, we will also live with Him; If we endure, we will also reign with Him; If we deny Him, He also will deny us; If we are faithless, He remains faithful, for He cannot deny Himself* (2 Tim 2:11-13, NASB).

He is a God who still beckons and asks that we build a heart for Him. God is yearning for us to be acceptable houses for Him to dwell in. We are living, precious stones in the sight of God that are designed to be spiritual sacrifices to the Lord. When you think about your heart, think about it as a collection of stones that represent your spirit and soul. Our hearts house the reality of what we believe in the kingdom of God. If your heart is built on flesh, you will carry out the actions of the flesh. If your heart is built on the spirit, you will carry out the deeds of the spirit.

> *As you come to him, a living stone rejected by men but in the sight of God chosen and precious, you yourselves like living stones are being built up as a spiritual house, to be a holy priesthood, to offer spiritual sacrifices acceptable to God through Jesus Christ.* (1 Pet. 2:4-5, ESV).

God's desire is for us to place our trust in Him. People will consistently reject us, but God welcomes us into His family as a holy royalty that is set apart. In order for us to be set apart though, we must be acceptable to God. I know that sounds crazy, who decides what is acceptable to God? If you are reading this book you can note that I have spent some time using Scripture as my foundation for my thoughts. Scripture is our explicit validation of what is acceptable to God. In order to build a house for God, we must build our house on Scripture. Everything else is sinking sand.

When I first came into the faith I did not understand the validity of Scripture. While riding in a car with our bible study leader, I made a comment that seemed to add to the Bible. He was extremely gracious with my knowledge-less zeal. I was a baby in Christ and I was barely drinking the milk (basic doctrines) of the faith. How arrogant of me to think that I could add to the Word of God? But that is what some of us do. We think we can add to the Word of God or question the wisdom of God simply because a specific topic such as abortion, cloning, or nuclear war is not addressed. Too many of us reason our way out of issues by ignoring the biblical correction the Holy Spirit, a leader in the church, or another person gives you. These are our issues of the heart and they often expose the foundation of our hearts.

Author and minister Brennan Manning was a believer who helped many of us understand the furious longing of God. Manning gives us glorious illustration of the love of God: "The foundation of the furious longing of God is the Father who is the originating Lover, the Son who is the full self-expression of that Love, and the Spirit who is the original and inexhaustible activity of that Love, drawing the created universe into itself."[27] God is the Creator of the universe and He furiously longs to be the foundation of our hearts.

First Things First

God is forever drawing us closer to His love. One of the key ways that God draws us into His love is through His Word. The Word of God is how we discover the attributes of our exuberant Lover. Digging into God's Word is how we dig into God's heart and build our hearts on His love. In order to build a house, you must first lay a foundation. Our current foundations are faulty and unstable. We have built our houses on sinking sand instead of His Word.

The greatest way to begin to receive and understand God's Word as a single person is through prayer. If the Word is our entryway into God's heart, prayer is the key that opens the door to God's heart. Many people approach God's Word without praying first and in doing so, miss the keyhole.

Without prayer we are searching around in the dark trying to find the opening. When you are in the dark you can't find the key, let alone the knob.

Studying the Bible isn't a task, it is a gift. One that should be received by praying first. When you pray, it allows God to speak to you but also builds a house of dependency. You can have all the tools, notebooks, highlights, pens, and desire in the world but none of it matters unless you pray first. Prayer is a place of two-way communication between you and God. In order to build a heart for God, we must first speak to God. God is longing to hear our voices. He longs for us to see that He hears us when we pray. God desires for us to be sitting off the edge of our seats waiting to hear the next Words that come out of His mouth and resonate in our hearts.

The word *pray* is mentioned 398 times in the KJV Bible and *prayer* is mentioned 138 times. Those numbers alone show its significance.

Prayer requires three key ingredients:

1. Communication with God
2. Belief in God
3. Waiting for response from God

The Eerdman's Bible Dictionary describes prayer as, "any form of communication with God on the part of believing people in response to situations that may arise in life.[28] In order to pray you must believe that Jesus is Lord. When I was new in the faith, the concept of Jesus as Lord clicked for me. I made a decision that summer of my junior year that I would follow God. Over the next month I spent time in prayer, the Word, Christian books, churches, video sermons etc. I was doing all the right things. Things I *thought* a Christian was supposed to do. However, I had yet to receive victory over my marijuana and masturbation addictions. While I was doing all the Christian activities, I knew God wasn't pleased with these activities because they weren't bearing fruit in my life. I knew I wanted God. I'd confessed that Jesus was Lord. I knew God existed but I'd left out one key element. I didn't pray to Jesus, I prayed to God. I wasn't taking the proper route. Before I prayed one morning on my basement floor, I remembered John 14:6:

> *"Jesus said to him, "I am the way, and the truth, and the life; no one comes to the Father but through Me. "If you had known Me, you would have known My Father also; from now on you know Him, and have seen Him"* (John 14:6-7 NASB)

Jesus is the door to our prayers being answered. When we rebuild our hearts for the Lord, we give Jesus open access to molding us into His image. The amazing thing about prayer is that no matter how terrible the circumstances, everything will work together for our good. We know that God causes all things to work together for good to those who love God, to those who are called according to *His* purpose (see Rom 8:28 NASB).

When we communicate with Jesus we are submitting to the plan He has for us. The purpose of prayer is to hear the response of God—not simply to speak to Him. "When we leave our place of prayer, we should be expecting God's answer. God doesn't want us walking around with attitudes of fear and doubt, wondering if He will do anything about our requests."[29] Do you feel inadequate before you read or study the Word? Well that is why we pray. We pray to remove our own thoughts and replace them with the peace of God.

As a single woman, I had many concerns about my courtship and possible marriage. When I finally decided to pray for my future unknown husband, an unexplainable grace and comfort came over me. I began to realize that God knew the plans He had for me and that through prayer, I got to wait expectantly to hear those plans if not at that moment but in minutes, hours, days, months, or even years to come.

Types of Prayer

There are several types of prayer:

A. Thanksgiving
B. Confession, imprecation (e.g., Num. 16:15; Ps. 69:22-28)
C. Nonverbal communication (Rom. 8:26),
D. Glossolalia (tongues) (1 Cor. 14:14-15)[30]

> *Lord, inspire us to read your Scriptures and to meditate upon them day and night. We beg you to give us real understanding of what we need, that we in turn may put its precepts into practice. Yet we know that understanding and good intentions are worthless, unless rooted in your graceful love. So we ask that the words of Scripture may also be not just signs on a page, but channels of grace into our hearts. Amen. (Prayer Attributed to Origen)*

Invite Him in

When we are building the foundations of our hearts, these are the ways that we can communicate to God. The next step is what I mentioned before, the Word. We pray because we believe that God's Word is true. His Word confirms the forward movement of our hearts and the words that are spoken by God in prayer. Without the Word of God, our spiritual houses are built on sinking sand and not the chief cornerstone. How hungry are you to have Jesus over to your home? In Luke 19, we receive one of the biggest illustrations of a heart that yearns to see Jesus.

> *He entered Jericho and was passing through. And there was a man called by the name of Zaccheus; he was a chief tax collector and he was rich. Zaccheus was trying to see who Jesus was, and was unable because of the crowd, for he was small in stature. So he ran on ahead and climbed up into a sycamore tree in order to see Him, for He was about to pass through that way. When Jesus came to the place, He looked up and said to him, "Zaccheus, hurry and come*

down, for today I must stay at your house." And he hurried and came down and received Him gladly. (Luke 19:1-6 NASB)

Zaccheus was a rich man who longed to see what all the fuss was about with Jesus. Imagine the street being crowded at an outside concert and in order to see, you have to climb a 100-foot tree (the average size of a sycamore tree is 98-130 feet). The width of the tree is about 6 feet wide. This was no small task for Zaccheus. In addition to climbing the tree, he was a rich man and known sinner in the community. He risked his reputation to see Jesus.

When we encounter the Word of God we are risking our reputation because we are conforming to His image. The image of Jesus is not widely received by the popular culture. Although crowds were around Jesus, He was still not widely accepted by the community. Calvary is proof of that. So are you really ready to be transformed in the image of God? If you are, then you have to be willing to climb up the tree to see Jesus. You have to be prepared to be called down and be willing to dine with Him in your spiritual home, your heart.

We pray before reading the Word so our hearts are primed to encounter the truth of the gospel and the instructions of the Holy Spirit. Many have called the Holy Spirit a still, small voice. The concept behind the still, small voice is that we must be attentive and listening in order to hear God. Many people are looking for signs and wonders. Signs are needed by an *unbelieving* generation according to Luke 11:29. But Jesus is looking for those who are yearning not for a sign but for an encounter with Him through His Word by way of the Holy Spirit.

David Watson was an evangelist in the U.K. known for using the arts to spark renewal and revival among the youth of the 1960s and 1970s. He stated, "Until the Holy Spirit illumines our dull minds and warms our cold hearts, we can not receive God's revealed truth, no matter how accurately we know the right words and teach them to others."[31]

As a single person, Jesus showed us in scripture the place of the Word of God in our lives. While in the wilderness after a 40-day fast, satan tempted Him with none other than the Word of God. When satan tempted Jesus, hungry and weary, He still proclaimed the Word of God. He answered and said, "It is written, 'Man shall not live on bread alone, but on every word that proceeds out of the mouth of God'" (Mt 4:4 NASB). If Jesus who is God in the flesh needed the Word of God while on this earth, how much more do we? God's Word is necessary to build our heart house properly. You want to be married? Grow in the Word of God. The sure fire way of overcoming the anxiety of singleness is building a heart for God. If we neglect the Word we neglect our ability to grow in Christ and reflect His image.

Back to Life

The Word of God is paramount to our lives. It is the light beneath our feet that gives us direction regarding all the affairs of our lives. David cried out, "Your word is a lamp to my feet and a light to my path. I have sworn and I will confirm it, that I will keep Your righteous ordinances. I am exceedingly afflicted; Revive me, O Lord, according to Your word (Ps 119:105-107 NASB). Reading and studying the Word of God is where our revival takes place. When we think about our hearts and minds, we must understand that everything in it needs to be renewed. We aren't building hearts for God because we need something to do. We are building hearts for God because we are broken. We are busy about everything else and we are missing one thing—a heart controlled by the Holy Spirit.

The biblical story of Mary and Martha is a great example of being busy about good things but not the right things. As Jesus was sitting around teaching the disciples and Mary, Martha was distracted. Martha was more concerned with caring for Jesus than sitting up under Jesus. Jesus didn't harshly rebuke Martha. Instead He graciously revealed the issue of her heart: "Martha, Martha, you are worried and bothered about so many things; but *only* one thing is necessary, for Mary has chosen the good part, which shall not be taken away from her" (Luke 10:41-42 NASB).

Jesus desires for us to come and sit under him and forget the cares of this world. The Word is our gate to hearing the heart of Jesus and not just the letters written in red. Whether you're new to the faith or a veteran, staying in the Word of God is always a battle. The enemy loves nothing more than to distract us; to get us to choose the issues of the world over spending time with the Lord in prayer and the Word.

Don't be condemned

Condemnation comes quite frequently concerning our time in the Word and with God. However, Jesus never condemned His disciples concerning their lack of faith or spending time with Him. What He did do was correct their thought processes and question their actions. If you have felt condemned or given your heart over to the distractions of this world, repent and move forward. Paul writes in Romans one of the most comforting verses. He says, "There is now no condemnation for those who are in Christ Jesus" (Rom 8:1 NASB). The peace of God is available to us all. We have been bought with a price and been given grace over every weakness. Our responsibility as believers is to allow the Lord to fill the dormant place of our hearts with the Word. Our minds need to be renewed concerning the importance of the Word of God in our growth.

When Paul encouraged the Romans not to be conformed by the world he was speaking of the worldly thought patterns.

> *And do not be conformed to this world, but be transformed by the renewing of your mind, so that you may prove what the will of God is, that which is good and acceptable and perfect.* (Ro 12:2 NASB)

The word *renewed* in the Greek is the word *anakaínōsis*. It means to renew qualitatively.[32] The measure by which we are renewed qualitatively is based on how renovated our minds are from the past. Imagine your friend boasting about their home renovation. Your mind would imagine that the home is completely different. Walls, doors, kitchen sink, ripped out and replaced by new appliances, sanded floors and some new future if not all. Now picture yourself walking into your friends' home and the only thing they changed was the couch. Would you call that a renovation or a new couch? I would likely graciously compliment my friend on the couch and then ask when the renovation will take place? Renovation is a renewal of something old to something new. Removing the old thoughts and replacing them with the Word of God creates a change in our minds. It's during this renewal that we experience an ocean of grace.

Oceans Deep

> *In Him we have redemption through His blood, the forgiveness of our trespasses, according to the riches of His grace which He lavished on us. In all wisdom and insight He made known to us the mystery of His will, according to His kind intention which He purposed in Him.* (Eph. 1:7-9 NASB)

An ocean of grace is found in the revealing of the mystery of God's will in His Word. When God gave us access to salvation, He gave us access to the mystery of His Word. There are many who attempt to read the Bible out of the flesh and end up with nothing but confusion and more questions. When you are in Jesus, you are therefore privy to the thoughts of God. As the Word renews our hearts, we begin to better understand why our hearts need the Word, prayer, fellowship and God's plan for our lives. It's not enough for us to simply pray and read the Word; we must be changed by the power of the Holy Spirit. The purpose of prayer and the Word is for us to be changed within. It is an act of restoration that can then flow into our lives and fellowship. Prayer is not independent of the Word and the Word is not independent of prayer.

Learn to pray before, during, and after your reading of the Scriptures. Prayer is especially crucial when you come to a place in your study where you are stuck and confused. That's a good time to stop and carry on a conversation with God. "Lord, I can't make any sense out of this passage. I don't understand it. Give me insight. Help me to discover Your truth."[33] There will be many moments in your singleness when you will feel far away from God. You might even be tempted to find temporary comforts that will feel close but lead you away from God. When adversity shows up, turn to the Lord in prayer and the Word.

Do you have heart issues that you don't understand? The Word of God is available to you to work out those issues. Our success in life comes from our time in the Word. At the beginning of a battle, God encouraged Joshua not only to be strong and courageous but also to set His hope day and night in the commandments of God.

> *"This book of the law shall not depart from your mouth, but you shall meditate on it day and night, so that you may be careful to do according to all that is written in it; for then you will make your way prosperous, and then you will have success* (Jos 1:8 NASB).

Some theologians say that to meditate on the Word means to mutter it over and over. The act of muttering means to speak in low, hushed tones. When we mutter the Word we are speaking to ourselves. Do you want success in your life? Mutter the Word of God. For example, if you are dealing with worry you can use Matthew 6:32 as a Scripture to meditate (mutter) on. *For the Gentiles eagerly seek all these things; for your heavenly Father knows that you need all these things* (Matt 6:32 NASB). As you mutter, God will begin to highlight specific words that you should then focus on. As I muttered this verse I focused on "Father knows." It brought a deep peace to my heart to know that my heavenly Father knows what I need. He isn't off in the distance not knowing my spiritual, emotional, and physical needs. He is in me and knows my cares and concerns. Even before I pray or read the Word, God knows what I have need of. God cares and is concerned for us.

Wow! The God of the universe cares for you and me. That right there can be a meditation! No matter how far off we are or how much we are struggling in anxiety, God knows and cares. He isn't looking at you as an anxious single. He is looking at you as a single that He desires to become intimately acquainted with; one who spends their time devoted to Him.

We too often pray that God will change our circumstances instead of praying that God draw us nearer to His presence. In the presence of God, we come into the reality that circumstances don't matter—He is with us. The reality of his presence can seem difficult to grasp when you are in a battle. Far too often circumstances make people skeptical of God's presence in the midst of suffering. How many times have you inwardly asked, *God where are you?* or *God will I ever get married?* or the classic, *God, if you love me, why am I going through this?* The focus is on ourselves and our battle instead of God and His ability to be with us in the midst of that battle. Jesus isn't a genie who snaps His finger and removes all the pain, sickness, and circumstances of the world. He is a God who provides peace in the midst of the storm and reminds you that He cares and knows your needs.

During a time of crisis, the greatest comfort is to know that the Lord is with you. Regardless of the outcome, you know that God has your back. To be in God's presence is to be in His sight. When you are in the midst of something hard, you need to stand in the presence of the Lord and know that God will fight your battle. Acknowledging that we are unable to fight is a huge step. We learn to depend on the Lord to win it for us.

The presence of God is not an emotional, fluffy state. It can be tangible when it's His manifest presence. Most times, the presence I'm referencing is an awareness that we are in the sight of God at all times. There is no place that we can go to be out of His sight. Nurture that sense in your soul. When you are focused on the presence of God, the circumstances don't matter. When we can identify and walk in the fullness of Jesus' desire to protect us and give us life, we are able to see Him in any circumstance.

> *I am the door; if anyone enters through Me, he will be saved, and will go in and out and find pasture. The thief comes only to steal and kill and destroy; I came that they may have life, and have it abundantly* (John 10:9–10 NASB).

One of the ways in which I combat my own thoughts of God not being with me is to repeat His Word and promise back to myself. For example, I've had a lot of financial difficulties while following my dreams. It has led to many moments of remembering that God is faithful even when my bank account is not. I've noticed that there is always a bird around to remind me that if He cares for the birds and the grass in the park, He will surely care for me. I repeat to myself, *if God feeds the birds, I'm surely not going hungry* (see Matthew 6:25). If Jesus is the door, why would He close the door on me during my hard times? If Jesus came to give me life, why would He withhold anything good from me? If Jesus isn't the thief, then why would I not receive His abundant life? Asking myself those questions reminds me of the promises of God and His nearness in the midst of my adversity. Instead of asking God where He is, we should be asking God why aren't we aware of His presence. The word *abundantly* is *perissós*, it means over and above, more than enough.[34] Just because you don't feel His presence in your prayer and Word time doesn't mean that you have not been given more than enough life. Jesus doesn't hold back His love from us. He is in the business of exceeding our expectations.

> *Now to Him who is able to do far more abundantly beyond all that we ask or think, according to the power that works within us, to Him be the glory in the church and in Christ*

Jesus to all generations forever and ever. Amen. (Eph. 3:20 NASB)

If Jesus is able to do over and above our expectations, what purpose would He have in withholding anything from us? The apostle Paul was a brave example of what it meant to know Christ. He looked at His circumstances as an opportunity and not a punishment.

He realized that when he and others "were so utterly, unbearably crushed that we despaired of life itself," it was to 'make us rely not on ourselves but on God who raises the dead,' adding, "he delivered us from so deadly a peril, and he will deliver us; on him we have set our hope that he will deliver us again.[35]"

The revelation that Jesus is for us and not against us offers us all confidence to move forward in any circumstance. Recently, I had a life changing conversation with one of the men who provides maintenance services in my office. I offered this gentleman coffee and we began to speak about his former life. In his former life, he was a satan worshipper. He devoted his life to evangelizing and bringing destruction to people. As we continued to talk, he spoke about coming to Jesus and now having to have his mind renovated to the gospel. We spoke about the power of prayer, how Christians don't realize the nearness of God, and the protection of angels. He asked, "How many angels do you think are around you right now?"

I responded, "I don't know maybe 10."

He then began to speak of the legions of angels that are assigned to each believer and that when believers pray, God opens up the heavens and sends legions of angels to our situations. My analytical mind was blown and I immediately went to Scripture to support the illustration. There were many instances where God used angels but what blew me the most was Matthew 26:53. It reads, "Or do you think that I cannot appeal to my Father, and He will at once put at my disposal more than twelve legions of angels?" In this instance, the chief priest's goon was taking Jesus and Peter slashed the goon's ear attempting to protect Him. Jesus instantly flexed His authority in the Spirit reminded Peter of His ability to call forth angels if needed. When we are in need of protection, God calls forth His angels to protect us. Psalm 91:11 says, "For He will give His angels charge concerning you, to guard you in all your ways." When I discovered these verses and combined them with the maintenance man's illustration, it blew my mind.

God hears us when we pray and puts legions of angels around us to protect us in the spirit realm. There is absolutely no need to fear because God is protecting us at all cost. We must build our hearts on God's truth and not on our doubts. He is in the business of caring for us and preparing us as His living stones into a royal priesthood. As we focus on prayer, the Word and fellowship God forms in our hearts reveals mysteries only His chosen can understand.

You are not single because there is something wrong with you. You are single because God has chosen this time for you to be groomed into His image and that is not a small matter. When you are married, your attentions are divided in caring for your spouse. It's not that you won't spend time with the Lord and grow in Jesus but your focus isn't dead on. Right now, you're single and you have nothing but time to allow the Lord to expose your weaknesses and build your strengths. Determine that today you will no longer be bound by your anxiety but use every opportunity to build your heart for God with no other distractions.

AN EXERCISE IN REFLECTION

Let's take some time to reflect on prayer. What are some of your prayer request?

_____
_____
_____
_____
_____
_____
_____
_____
_____
_____

Using Ephesians 3:20 as the backdrop to the prayers above, tweet me @christinafaith and share what you are believing God for in your life so I can pray with you.

Chapter Seven

The Identity Question: Love is Who You Are

I'm a lover. I love people. But I wasn't always like that. There's a significant difference between engaging people to put on a show like you care and really *caring* for them. When I was single, I made it a goal of mine to ask people how they were doing as an act of love. When people would give me simple answers, I'd remind them, "I'm asking because I really want to know." Most people don't really want to know how someone is doing. The question is perfunctory, at best. But if I wanted to learn to love well, I knew I needed to be concerned with and for people.

As a single my focus shifted to love. I have spoken quite a bit about our sins and the emotional state of singles. The amazing reality of God is that He reveals all of our flaws in order to express His deep love for us. He is not like our parents who have to cool down before they deal with our mistakes. God loves us with a true unconditional love, and His love can only be duplicated by those who are deeply in love with Him.

God's love for us isn't predicated on our love for Him. Jesus expressed His deep love for us with His death. Romans

5:8 expresses this loving reality: "But God demonstrates His own love toward us, in that while we were yet sinners, Christ died for us." The Greek word for *love* here is ἀγάπη or *agape* — it means to love[36]. If you have been in the Kingdom of God, you have probably heard *agape* used a lot.

Love in our culture has been so fabricated. The word doesn't hold the same weight as in biblical times. *I love you* too often means *I lust you*. This is because love can be expressed in affection, benevolence, sensuality, or desire. Love is overused and misused all the time.

Jesus' love does not care about what you desire. His love is based on what He desires to give us.[37] When God expressed His love in the form of agape toward us, it was like a love feast. The early church enjoyed love feasts. At a love feast, the wealthy Christians would foot the bill for an all-you-can-eat banquet where Jesus was honored by the serving of communion and no one was treated differently because of how much money they had or where they were from. The poor Christians didn't have to worry about how they were going to eat, because the wealthy Christians were so rich in love that they covered their brothers and sisters' financial weakness.

The love feast represented God's love toward us. When we love each other we show others the love of God and they know we are His. The essence of a Christian's ability to love another is based on God's love towards them. But here's the catch: our love is based on Jesus' ability to love us but Jesus ability to love us has nothing to do with our love for Him. God's love is His currency. "The God of love" means He's the author and source of love.[38] Without Him, our wounds stay wounds and never heal. The supreme focus of the Kingdom of God is love and for a single man or woman, this is a comforting thought to remember. It is the very character and make up of God. "Love is so essential that we are nothing without it.[39]"

As Christians, our identity is wrapped in the love of God. We cannot reflect Jesus to anyone, especially a spouse, without the lavishly loving God. We can't work to reflect this identity. We can't even repent of our sins without the love of God. "All of my irritating sins are covered by the cross where Jesus died for my sins. Your sins are covered too, because of the love of Jesus.[40]" If we are working on not being anxious about our lives, then we must learn to die daily to our own desires so that we may rest in the love and peace of God.

In truth, love can be a humiliating topic to write about. No human being on earth loves perfectly. When we read 1 Corinthians 13, we can clearly see how we fall short of bearing all things. I recognize even now, areas where I could have loved someone deeper. Yet, seeing how deeply God loves us and gives us His amazing grace shows me that despite my imperfect love, I can continually reach out my hand to demonstrate love over and over.

As a believer, my identity is love. As a believer, your identity is love. The identity of love does not change with your marital status. Instead, being married puts you in a position to see a daily mirror of how much you do or don't love. If the very characteristic of God is love, how much should we expect that *our* primary characteristic is to be love?

While praying to the Father one morning, Jesus lifted up His eyes and prayed about us. His time had come and He was expressing His heart about His time on earth. He glorified the Father while He was here and was preparing to seal the deal of our eternal lives. After asking the Father many things on our behalf, Jesus began to close his prayer.

> *The glory which You have given Me I have given to them, that they may be one, just as We are one; I in them and You in Me, that they may be perfected in unity, so that the world may know that You sent Me, and loved them, even as You have loved Me.* (John 17:22-23 NASB)

Jesus was consumed with love for us and desired that we be perfected in unity. We know that our identity is found only in Jesus' love because that's where His identity was found in the Father. Love was the reason Jesus came. Love was the reason Jesus died. Jesus was all about love because the love of the Father was in Him. We are able to love because the love of Jesus is in us. Jesus proclaimed, "I have made Your name known to them, and will make it known, so that the love with which You loved Me may be in them, and I in them" (John 17:26 NASB). The love of God is inside of you if you have accepted Him as Savior. As a single person, we sometimes think the most comforting is the love of a significant other. Significant others are the icing on the cake, but they are not the actual cake.

When It Hurts So Bad

100% of our healing is about pulling out old thought processes, wrong motivations, hidden sin, and any other issues that stop us from experiencing the love of God. Jesus' love isn't based on how we feel. Jesus' love is based on what He did. He loved us therefore we can love. He loved us because we need an unconditional love that doesn't allow circumstances to change the way we are loved. "Jesus treats us the same loving way. He does not get impatient with our misguided questions or angry about our repeated mistakes. He comes to us in love, kindly correcting us, patiently explaining the way of salvation, graciously cleansing us, and humbly serving our every need.[41]"

I recently began to consider my identity prior to Jesus coming into my heart. My identity was formed around my family, schooling, things I owned, things I knew and the locations I was from. As a child, we moved quite often. We moved so much that my geographical identity was always the state, not a particular town or city. When people asked me where I was from, I said, "New Jersey." A huge part of my identity was ironically, wrapped around not having an identity at all. My identity was formed specifically around what I knew. The ways in which I could get out of trouble. The things I had materially that allowed me to make friends with a kid in each new school. Yet, when I found Jesus, none of that stuff mattered anymore. My identity then became my faith. I was a Christian. In Jesus, I found where I belonged and no one could take that identity away from me. My identity was then and is now wrapped in Jesus' ability to love and mold me in His image.

When Jesus welcomed us into His kingdom and we accepted His love, we signed up to be shaped into His image. We signed up to take on that image. The anxiety that too many of us have regarding our singleness is all about how we see ourselves. Every action we take in life has an identity formation question behind it. How we see ourselves matters.[42] Every thought we think is wrapped in how we see ourselves. Do you see yourself as the bride of the King who loves you? Is Jesus enough for you? Is His love all consuming to you?

When you see yourself through the eyes of the bride, you get a glimpse of what was given in order for you to love Jesus and be loved by Him. Captivated by Jesus' ability to forgive sins the woman with the alabaster box came to a Pharisees home where Jesus was dining and wept. She didn't weep because she felt condemned by her sins. She wept because she knew by faith that Jesus was going to forgive her. The woman knew the debt of her sins and that they were many. Let's walk through this in Luke 7:36-50. The theme of this passage is regarding debt. In verse 37, the woman is introduced as a sinner. Just imagine what it would feel like to know that your sins are so abundant that your entire community knows you for them. We all know people who are known by their sins. She was a woman who had a great need for forgiveness. Immediately when she came into the house, she began to weep. Her tears were so abundant that they were enough to clean Jesus' feet. Along with her tears, she brought an alabaster box full of oil to anoint His feet. The woman had absolutely no shame. She knew of the forgiveness that Jesus held that she risked her reputation even more to clean his feet with her wealth (oil) and tears of gratitude.

The Pharisee, of course, did not approve of her actions and questioned Jesus' status as a prophet because of it. Luke 7:39 says, "Now when the Pharisee who had invited Him saw this, he said to himself, 'If this man were a prophet He would know who and what sort of person this woman is who is touching Him, that she is a sinner.'" Imagine that! You invited Jesus to your home and then you insult him because he embraced a sinner. Jesus was smooth though. In response, he offered an analogy:

> *And Jesus answered him, "Simon, I have something to say to you." And he replied, "Say it, Teacher." "A moneylender had two debtors: one owed five hundred denarii, and the other fifty. "When they were unable to repay, he graciously forgave them both. So which of them will love him more?" Simon answered and said, "I suppose the one whom he forgave more." And He said to him, "You have judged correctly." Turning toward the woman, He said to Simon, "Do you see this woman? I entered your house; you gave Me no water for My feet, but she has wet My feet with her tears and wiped them with her hair. "You gave Me no kiss; but she, since the time I came in, has not ceased to kiss My feet. "You did not anoint My head with oil, but she anointed My feet with perfume. "For this reason I say to you, her sins, which are many, have been forgiven, for she loved much; but he who is forgiven little, loves little." Then He said to her, "Your sins have been forgiven." (Luke 7:40-48 NASB)*

The woman understood her debt. It was her debt that caused her to weep and anoint Jesus' feet. However, the Pharisee could not see that because He was unaware of the debt of sin that he also carried himself. Both owed a debt and both were graciously forgiven. However, the one who carried the highest debt appreciated the forgiveness more. When Jesus came into a home, it was customary for the host to offer water to clean a guest's—especially a prophet's—feet. But the Pharisee didn't regard Jesus as a prophet. He regarded Jesus as a common guest. The Pharisee actually probably invited Jesus to find out more information regarding the man whom the people called a prophet.

The woman was forgiven much because she was the person with the highest debt in the room. She lived a life of shame, guilt, and condemnation by her community. She loved Jesus based on her need for forgiveness. She knew the value of Jesus' love and that love caused her to weep with gratitude and appreciation. The words *loved* and *loves* in verse 46 is *agapáō*. There's that word again!

Agape is not only unconditional love but an esteeming of love that finds joy in someone. Agape can be described as, "to esteem, love, indicating a direction of the will and finding one's joy in something or someone." [43] The woman with the alabaster box found her place of joy and that caused her to love much. So consider this: As a single person does Jesus' forgiving love cause you to love much? When you look at people whose sin is commonly known do you look at them with love or disgust? The greatest thing a single or married believer can do is learn how to love much. Love the Lord much because He has forgiven us deeply. Love people much because *we* have been forgiven deeply.

Imagine the peace that came over this woman after she had given all that she had in tears and oil to hear that her sins had been forgiven. She was forgiven based on her faith in the one who she anointed. No one told her that Jesus carried forgiveness. She believed by faith that Jesus could heal her hurting heart and restore her dignity. The Pharisee couldn't understand how Jesus could forgive her for her sins. But the woman understood by the Spirit of Christ that He was the forgiver. When you are forgiven of much you tend to be more vocal about what God has saved you from. When you are unaware of your need of forgiveness you are baffled by one who has been forgiven.

Jesus said to the woman, "Your faith has saved you; go in peace."[44] Instead of walking away with her head low, she went away in the abundant peace of forgiveness. If we had to picture this peace, we might imagine that it looks like a woman with a hole in her heart and that hole finally being filled. When she walked away, her heart was now whole and it beat according to the love of God's forgiveness and not the snares of her community.

When you have received an abundance of forgiveness, you put out an abundance of love. It was around 2007 when I realized I had a serious problem with love. I didn't love like Jesus loved. Sitting in my Christian therapist's office, she asked me, "What's on your heart today?" I began to weep and say, "I want to love like Jesus does." My love life had been so flawed growing up. I loved people but I didn't love them with the unconditional love of Jesus. I had been one who was deeply wounded and I put up walls everywhere. I put up so many walls that God had to break me. I had to learn how to love with no barriers. I needed to learn how to love and not hold anything against people. My therapist didn't say anything profound that I can remember but she did usher in peace. The peace I received was because my desire to love like God did was driving my process. I am now one who loves hard. I hold no partiality when it comes to loving people. I love a stranger the same way I love a friend. But here's the point: I love that way because I've been forgiven greatly!

A part of my journey to learning how to love as a child of God has been facilitated by people. Our love for God is attached to our love of God's people. The original commandment in Deuteronomy 6:5 is directly related to our love for God. Jesus left one command for us that covered all the 10. He said, "You shall love the Lord your God with all your heart, and with all your soul, and with all your strength, and with all your mind; and your neighbor as yourself" (Luke 7:50 NASB). If we love the Lord with all we have then we will love ourselves rightly and, in turn, be able to love our neighbor as ourselves.

When I moved in with my roommate Olivia, it was my desperate desire to walk by faith and love. I had been so used to living my own life and serving people at a distance that I truly wanted to love someone through all the junk that comes from relationship. The amazing thing about God is that He has a humorous way of preparing us for our spouses. You see Olivia and my husband are very similar. I learned a lot of about loving my husband by loving Olivia. As my sister, she often encourages me by reflecting on how much I love her, but I know that's only because the Lord taught me how.

1st Corinthians 13 became extremely clear to me while living with Olivia. She was my training ground for actually loving someone and not hiding behind my emotions. The people of Corinth were not loving each other. This is why Paul wrote this "love chapter" as it is commonly known. When he says, "love bears all things," it can get a prickly for us. I know it did for me. I had to learn what it meant to bear all things. In my family, we loved each other by fighting. But that wasn't Olivia's way. When she chose to shut down, like in the case of Yogurt-gate, it was hard. Where I was from, we addressed things head on. One time, after 10 days of her silent treatment, I went into her room and made her talk to me. I noticed that the enemy was using the offense to divide us. It was the exact opposite of love.

I am not one who likes to confront people so this was hard for me. Confrontation requires that you put it all on the line and leave it there. The Word of God encourages us to take our offenses to our brothers and I didn't want to. Besides in my family, we just screamed at each other so confrontation for me equated to trauma. However, I was more concerned with my heart and hers. Yes, Love bears all things, including silence, but love does not allow division to continue to exist. We were both two wounded women living together and we needed deep doses of love. How could I speak to other people about their need to allow Jesus in their hearts while having issues with my sister?

The Lord exposed our hearts and showed us that we both needed to learn how to love deeper. Jesus loves us with this amazing agape love that we often take for granted. We take it for granted because we are more willing to receive it from Jesus but aren't as quick to return it to our brother or sister. Paul got us together though:

> *Love is patient, love is kind and is not jealous; love does not brag and is not arrogant, does not act unbecomingly; it*

> *does not seek its own, is not provoked, does not take into account a wrong suffered, does not rejoice in unrighteousness, but rejoices with the truth; bears all things, believes all things, hopes all things, endures all things. (1 Cor. 13:4-1)*

So in every circumstance of life we have to ask ourselves the following:

> *Am I being patient?*
> *Am I kind?*
> *Am I jealous?*
> *Am I arrogant?*
> *Am I acting unbecomingly?*
> *Am I seeking my own interest?*
> *Do I remember wrongs I suffered because of another?*
> *Am I rejoicing with sin?*
> *Do I rejoice with truth?*
> *Am I bearing ALL things?*
> *Do I really believe all things?*
> *Am I hoping all things?*
> *Am I enduring all things?*

More times than I'd like to admit, I am not doing any of these things. I often react out of my flesh and until I step back and evaluate my life and actions according to these principles of love, I walk in hate. When we measure our love based on these thirteen truths of love, it begins to open up our hearts to the proper measure of our love. Jesus stated, "A new commandment I give to you, that you love one another, even as I have loved you, that you also love one another. By this all men will know that you are My disciples, if you have love for one another" (John 13:34).

While we were courting, my husband Allen shut down similarly to the way Olivia did whenever we had drama. It drove me crazy because, once again, I felt rejected. Isn't it wild how we respond to a perceived lack of love? After several counseling sessions, Allen and I learned that he needed a few days to process things before he addressed them. I had to learn that love really is patient and to not hold the wrong I suffered against him. Thankfully, I had a taste of that prior to our courtship through Olivia.

Love is a verb and a noun. Love isn't love if it does not include an action, a *doing*. When Jesus died for us and rose from the dead, that was His way of showing us that He loves us. God's agenda is loving us and that love is expressed through infinite actions.

One of those loving action is correction.

Correction is frequently processed as rejection. As a child, I processed correction as rejection and so therefore, as an adult I did the same. I can remember one time with my father when he was supposed to be at the house with me and he was out getting high. My aunt came to pick me up from his mother's house and he passed us on his way back in. His lip was twisted from getting high and he smelled like what I now know to be crack. I was embarrassed. I don't have many memories of my father but 90% of them were of him choosing drugs over me or others he should have been loving. For me, his rejection translated into the message that I wasn't good enough.

When I first discovered the words of scripture concerning correction, I was amazed. In my dorm room, I read Hebrews 12:5-7 and cried out to the Lord, asking that He chasten (discipline, correct) me. I did not fully understand what I was crying out for but I knew that it said this is how He shows us that He loves me and I wanted to be deeply loved by God. In His correction, God expresses that He loves us. Read what Paul wrote to the Hebrews:

> *And have you forgotten the exhortation that addresses you as sons? "My son, do not regard lightly the discipline of the Lord, nor be weary when reproved by him. For the Lord disciplines the one he loves, and chastises every son whom he receives."* (Heb. 12:5–6 NASB)

When I processed those verses, I began to understand all of the punishments and reprimands my mother gave me in my life were for my good. During the time of the discipline, all I saw was rejection but, in actuality, my mother was showing me that she loved me by not allowing me to get away with harmful behaviors. Jesus is the exact same way. He loves us and wants to prune off of us our toxic behaviors so that we can learn how to love. Love requires the action of our hearts and hands. When we are disciplined for our lack of love, God is showing by His action of discipline that He loves us.

Every circumstance in our lives is for the purpose of shaping us. I've mentioned author Bob Goff earlier in the book. In his book *Love Does*, he states, "I used to think I could shape the circumstances around me, but now I know Jesus uses circumstances to shape me."[45] In every instance, I ask God to teach me how to love. When the opportunity to love comes up, I'm always challenged to dig deeper to reflect His loving heart and not depend on myself. When we have been hurt we tend to hold onto the hurt instead of allowing forgiveness to be led by love.

If Jesus forgave us but brought up what He forgave us of every time He had an issue with us, how would we feel? I don't know about you but I wouldn't want to speak to Jesus often. I'd probably put those walls up over and over again and not engage in relationship with Jesus. The thing is, we tend to think that forgiveness means forgetfulness and that is wrong. Forgiveness implies that we do not hold someone to an offense; we remit the offense. *The Complete Word Study Dictionary* provides a great definition of forgiveness: "To let go from one's power, possession, to let go free, let escape[46]".

Likewise, if my husband offends me, it is my responsibility to forgive my husband and then talk to him about the issue. When I forgive him, I am then responsible also not to hold the offense against him in my heart or in further conversation. If we don't forgive another, how then can we accept Christ's forgiveness of us? We are human beings with tender hearts and those tender hearts tend to lead how we forgive instead of our love for Jesus leading our forgiveness. Paul states in 2 Corinthians, "But one whom you forgive anything, I *forgive* also; for indeed what I have forgiven, if I have forgiven anything, *I did it* for your sakes in the presence of Christ" (2 Co 2:10 NASB).

A Deeper Love

There are so many things that can stop us from loving the way Jesus designed us to love. The forgiveness of others' sins against us doesn't mean that we will forget them. Remember the forgiveness of sins means that will not count those sins against the offender. When the woman with the alabaster box was forgiven, Jesus no longer held those sins against her. Although the community may have still remembered her past, she was able to walk away from her former sins because of Jesus' love. Although we might remember the affliction caused by another, we are called to forgive them in the midst of it. We can't pray away our sins. We must repent from them.

I want a deep well of love flowing through me. I don't want a love that is contingent upon sex and things that don't last. One thing married people will tell you is that sex is only a portion of their marriage, it is not the main event. Too many people are getting married for sex and companionship but the truth is, sex doesn't cure lust and marriage doesn't cure loneliness. Only a deep relationship with the Lord will bring peace in these circumstances.

When you think of your potential husband or wife, do you imagine them full of unforgiveness? Of course not! All of us hope that our mates will have healed from past relationships. Are you allowing the Lord to teach you how to love in order for you to be healed from those relationships as well?

Learning to love must be accompanied by learning to forgive. Love and forgiveness go hand and hand. If you have a problem loving, you have a problem forgiving. The worst thing anyone can do is enter a courtship with unresolved relational issues.

I have a friend, Margo, who began a relationship with Tommy. Tommy is a great guy and Margo is an awesome young lady. But two months into the relationship, I started to see signs of Margo being extremely insecure. When Tommy was having a conversation with a female friend, Margo would automatically become jealous. The next day, Margo would question Tommy about his conversation and interaction with his friend. Tommy never showed any signs of being unfaithful and his female friends were extremely supportive of their relationship. Unfortunately, Margo had been cheated on in the past and she saw Tommy through that same lens.

We have seen it over and over. We bring our old baggage into our new relationship. Thankfully, the love of God reveals, exposes, and provides the ointment to heal our hearts and teach us how to love. If we are to be citizens of the Kingdom, then our currency should be love. As I noted, God's agenda is loving us. Our agenda then, is loving Him and loving our neighbor as ourselves. We are deceiving ourselves if we think that one agenda can be accomplished without the other. I can't love God and have unresolved issues with people. If we are going to take on the identity of the kingdom we must receive the DNA of the kingdom as well. That DNA is love.

Love is an amazing gift that God has granted us. When God decided to love us, He decided to give us His love language. His love language knows no boundaries and is unconditional. There is nothing that can separate us from His love.

As a new believer, I posted scriptures all over my bathroom and bedroom to get the Word down in my heart. There is one scripture I memorized that continues to remind me of the magnitude of God's love:

> *For I am convinced that neither death, nor life, nor angels, nor principalities, nor things present, nor things to come, nor powers, nor height, nor depth, nor any other created thing, will be able to separate us from the love of God, which is in Christ Jesus our Lord.* (Rom 8:38-39 NASB).

Take Me As I Am

I've been thinking about what it means to be authentic for most of my life without knowing it. My interest in the concept was born from an extremely troubling time in my life. It wasn't troubling because of my circumstances. It was troubling because I'd shrunk into this hole called comparison. I had no idea I was in this hole though until I was in a classroom and was scheduled to preach. I stood up in front of 10 classmates and my professor and spoke from a manuscript.

It was the worst!

I don't even remember what the message was about. I do know that I was in a safe place. My classmates and professor all went around encouraging me. They knew that what I'd just done was not authentically me and that hurt!

It didn't hurt because I had put all my heart into that message and it didn't go well. It hurt because the feedback they were giving me was true. Preaching from a manuscript wasn't me. It was me trying to put myself in this box I'd manufactured all because of my insecurities.

The authentic me—the me that was clear about the love of Jesus being my identity—was birthed on a Sunday. I was going about my usual business of serving at church on the creative and technical team. I stood on the stage and looked at this young lady and said to myself, *she looks like she needs someone to talk to or a hug*. My first response to this thought was "Let me get Wanda to talk to her." Then the Holy Spirit slapped me in face. *You do it*. Those words shocked me because I realized right then and there that I'd stopped being me. I never had a problem talking to anyone. I'm the bold person. I'm the one friends send out to have those hard talks with people or to do something everyone else was afraid to do. It was in that instance this word "authentic" came to me. *Christina Faith, be authentic!* It was that simple. I knew right then that I had to be the person I was created to be. I almost cried that day because I thought about the previous four years and just how unauthentic I had become. I was jacked up! I believe the Holy Spirit spoke to me in that instance and it ignited something in me that I have not been able to shake since.

So I was scheduled to speak again in class the next week and, this time, with this new revelation, I was on a mission. I had to redeem myself and do what I knew to do. I knew what message I would bring this time and I had 10 minutes to speak on it. My goal was to ignite a revolution in the hearts of those 10 classmates and my professor. This time I got up there with my new iPad 2 and an outline. No manuscript. I am a terrible reading aloud. I always speak too fast. Why in the world did I try to speak from a manuscript anyway? The real me was way too impulsive and spontaneous to be confined to the words on a piece of paper. That day, I decided to speak from a place deep in my heart. It wasn't a place of superiority but a cry for a generation to wake up and be themselves.

After I delivered the message, I felt good. I got a rush. I got my mojo back. But my professor said something to me that day I won't forget. She said, "This is a message your generation, my generation and the world needs to hear. It isn't for a book or a few, it's for the world!"

I believed her! I was then asked to speak at a bible study that Wednesday. Guess what I taught on? You guessed it! The title was, "Authentic Me." After I finished, one of my closest friends told me I needed to make it the title of my album because people needed to hear it. That was so overwhelming. But it's also how I know that I could not approach the writing of this book from a place of "I got this all figured out."

I am writing it from a desperate place.

It makes me want to cry when I see people on a daily basis trying to be different; trying to fit in. They are searching and longing to be themselves but end up living as a carbon copy of the latest cultural fad or trend. They have no identity.

We live in a society where the majority of people do not know who they are. And contrary to what the world would have you believe, being authentic isn't about self-love. It's about self-discovery through this crazy thing called grace.

Being single and anxious is a result of having not yet discovered that much needed grace. On my journey, I didn't discover *me*. I discovered the *me inside of Him*—Jesus. And it was Jesus who took away my anxiety about being single. Being authentic has nothing to do with what you wear or how you look. Your identity doesn't lie in what type of music you listen to. Being authentic is all about discovering the well of love from this Lover of lovers that your heart is thirsty for.

What makes you, you? Every human being struggles to answer that question. We are all leveraging our entire lives on that one question. Our search for love, religion, attention, careers, fashion, food is all about that question. We aren't self-made individuals. We are a people created for specific purposes. And that jacks us all up! Ask yourself what does the "Authentic Me" look like? Why am I so afraid to be single? No, for real! How much of who you are is a fake? Who are you trying to be instead of just being you? How has that falseness worked out for you in relationships? See, life is about chemistry. It's a composition of people, places, and things. Far too often we experience failed compositions. We mix ourselves with things and people we shouldn't and our experiment blows up in our face. I am convinced that the perfect composition to being our authentic selves is when we are mixed with He—Jesus. That's the cure for anxiety.

AN EXERCISE IN REFLECTION

Let's take some time to reflect on our ability to forgive. Who do you need to forgive? Make a list of their names here.

_____

_____

_____

_____

_____

_____

A Prayer

Father God, it's crazy how you didn't just give us salvation, healing, and restoration but You just lavished it on us. Some of us don't know what it is to be lavished on. We see it, maybe even experience it, but we don't really get it. Your lavish love is like being submerged in a pool of the greatest healing water in the earth. You provide healing in places where nothing but your hyssop can reach. Thank you for your forgiveness. Your Word digs down deep and reaches us in the places that only you can see. You didn't just redeem us but You have provided ABUNDANTLY this incredible gift of sanctification. You put all the building blocks together for us to live a life of joy and eternal peace. Lord, Your riches are so deep that You don't have to give them out in tidbits but you give out more than even is needed. You don't just meet our needs but you give in excess to our needs. Your giving isn't one-dimensional. It's not just our finances, but you provide the very things we need in our spiritual and soul realms.

Help me, Jesus, to be more like You. Help me to have an unstoppable love and drink from Your well of forgiveness. Give me the courage and wisdom to move forward in Your grace and love. As You have lavished Your love on me, help me to lavish it on others as well. In Jesus' name, Amen.

Chapter Eight

Who's the Boss?

I know, I know. I'm not the boss of you. God is. This is a hard chapter for me to even begin. The crazy thing about many of the concepts and principles I am writing about is that I have not perfected them at all in my own life. However, I know I must write it and be convicted to change right along with you. Romans 13:1 states, "Every person is to be in subjection to the governing authorities. For there is no authority except from God, and those which exist are established by God." So you want to be married? Name a greater time to work on subjecting yourself to authority!

Let's define authority. As I mentioned, I came out of a bad church experience where the use of authority was abused and misused. It took some time to extract myself from that stronghold but I soon learned what the apostle Paul meant when he described how healthy authority should look. He writes: "For even if I boast somewhat further about our authority, which the Lord gave for building you up and not for destroying you" (2 Co 10:8 NASB). Healthy authority builds and does not destroy. The word *authority* here is the Greek word *exousia*. Exousia means to have power or authority over someone. Unfortunately, power can be abused and all too often we see the abuse of power and authority.

As a single person, I learned the value of submitting my will to another in creative work and collaborations. So when I write "submitting," I am not referring to abuse or misuse of power. If someone is abusing his or her authority and holding it over you, I pray you have the courage to leave that circumstance. Regarding spiritual authority, a healthy leader will be one who walks in God's authority refusing to tamper with the Word of God (see 2 Cor. 4:2 NASB).

Side note: If you feel that you are being abused spiritually feel free to email me and I will send you a freedom starter kit full of tools and resources to identify and verify those abuses cf@creativethoughtmedia.com

Submitting yourself to another in order to work together in unity is the ideal we should strive for. I am in no way referring to being a slave, a *yes man*, or not having opinion. Working with someone who is the lead of a project, organization, or planning can be hard because some people are not healthy leaders. But in nearly everything in life, someone has to lead.

Imagine being on a highway with two cars riding alongside each other. Everything is going grand, the roofs are down, each person is listening to their preferred music and they are communicating to each other through a Bluetooth headset. But there is a car in front of them. What happens if both cars keep going at the same speed? One of them gets into an accident. Maybe even both cars? However, what happens if the car on the right tells the car on the left to fall behind and follow? Accident avoided. Yes, they are equal cars. But if one of them does not take the lead, they will either get separated by the one car slowing down because they didn't want to fall back or they will keep at the same pace riding with each other on one accord. Proper leading will always build you up and not break you down It should leave you encouraged and inspired to take the next steps no matter how hard the next steps might be.

What does this have to do with singleness?

Unity and authority are two issues that have plagued relationships and marriages since Adam and Eve. Too often we fail to remember that this life is not about our preferences; our likes and dislikes. The evils of the world have been successful in separating and breaking down the fabric of our lives since that first encounter in the garden. Sometimes it hurts to let someone else lead or take the place we believe we should have. Rudy Huxtable was the youngest character on the hit television show, *The Cosby show*. In one episode, she gave us one of the greatest examples of the magnitude of human selfishness. While in music class, she was asked to play the triangle. She was not happy about this. She wanted to play the cymbals. As any child or adult would do when they can't get their way, she whined and got her choice. The problem with Rudy getting her way was this: she wasn't good at the cymbals. Her playing, based on her family's reactions was no love on the ears. But Rudy focused on what she wanted and didn't realize that she was an equal participant that mattered no matter what she played. A key point of Rudy's lesson was this: Her teacher knew in what area she was gifted but she didn't trust the leader. Rudy wanted her own way. Because of this, she diminished the unity—and sound—of her team and hurt her classmates' feelings. See, the beauty of unity is that we all have to die to ourselves in order to see it come to fruition. For Rudy, unity didn't come until after she decided to follow the direction of her teacher. During the closing scene, Rudy experienced joy beyond her imagination, learned the purpose of teamwork, and excelled in her given assignment—the triangle.

In a phrase, don't be a Rudy.

In singleness, it's important to learn how to operate as a team with those around you: friends, roommates, and (or) organizations. In marriage, everything is about teamwork. Just because you are figuratively playing the triangle and not the cymbals in your relationship, doesn't mean that you are any less than your partner. It simply means that, in that season, you are called to play a different instrument that also has significance.

Let's break down this concept of unity and authority. Singleness is a place of preparation for death. If you don't want to die, you've been reading the wrong book. I'm not talking about dying an earthly death but a death of brokenness and selflessness. A kind of death where you allow your pride to hit the floor. Much of the problems in relationships is no one is willing to die to self. We may not be in physically violent relationships but we wound each other emotionally and mentally with our pride. The purpose of your singleness is to work on being whole. That is also the purpose of unity.

> *...Until we all attain to the unity of the faith and of the knowledge of the Son of God, to mature manhood, to the measure of the stature of the fullness of Christ, so that we may no longer be children, tossed to and fro by the waves and carried about by every wind of doctrine, by human cunning, by craftiness in deceitful schemes. Rather, speaking the truth in love, we are to grow up in every way into him who is the head, into Christ, from whom the whole body, joined and held together by every joint with which it is equipped, when each part is working properly, makes the body grow so that it builds itself up in love.* (Eph. 4:13-16 NASB)

Chapter Nine

Die Empty

It has been my pleasure to write this book. This chapter is significant for me personally. Years ago, I declared to the Lord that I wanted to die empty. I wanted my life is be poured out according to His will and heart. There have been so many projects, plans and disappointments I have endured in my short three decades of life. The seeds of this book and the subsequent web series took place in 2008. In the midst of my singleness, I'd begun to realize that I was *Single and Anxious*, a battle that many of my friends were fighting as well. I had the pleasure of being connected to singles who, like me, longed to see the grace of God in their lives. The process wasn't easy but it was worth it. I can declare that, in my singleness, I emptied my life out for the Lord Jesus Christ. I'm not referencing accomplishments but that I served at the pleasure of Jesus Christ. He owned my life!

    I knew that I was under the hands of Jesus when he told me to leave my job in 2008. I had a good job. I had a house. I had a car. I had all the things a single woman in her twenties wanted. However, I had also declared that my life was not my own and that I would do whatever the Lord called of me. So at the age of 26, I left my good state job, house, and had my car repossessed. To the outside world, I looked crazy, but inside, where it mattered, I just wanted Jesus. I wanted everything that He had for me and I didn't want for it to ever to be said that I loved things more than I loved Jesus. During this period in my life, I journeyed to live by faith and not by sight. After all, my given name is Christina Faith.

In that season, I learned what it truly meant to follow Jesus. Through every hard place, the Lord exposed my nasty heart and my desperate need for Him. The latter hasn't stopped either. He is still doing that today. I am an unfinished vessel of the Lord that needs a lot of smoothing out still.

I created a graphic background for my computer and phone that simply stated, "Die Empty" with 2 Timothy 4:7 along the side. After I settled in my heart and mind that my life was not my own and my singleness belonged to God, that phrase became my focus. I no longer desired to waste thoughts and emotions on worrying about whether the next guy walking past or that friended me on Facebook was the one. I wanted to be focused on what God desired my life to look like.

When you are single and anxious, you have so much time on your hands and that time is often wasted. Think about how you have spent your singleness. How much of that time has been spent doing the work of God? Myles Munroe, an amazing minister of the gospel, who passed away along with 8 others in a plane crash in 2014, arguably, didn't die with regrets. He died empty. The evidence of this was found in the fact that he planted a flourishing church in the Bahamas, authored over 18 books, trained thousands of leaders and passed the baton to a ready leader (his son) upon his death. How many visions has the Lord given you that you have yet to complete?

I can say personally that I understand the struggle of completing a task. But that's what the Holy Spirit is for—to comfort and guide us. Whenever I fail to persist in completing what the Lord has put before me, it's due to a lack of time management, faith, confidence and sheer laziness. Even in the completion of this book, I have heard *die empty* echo in my own mind. I am not concerned with how it will sell but I am concerned with completing what the Lord has put in my hands to do for His glory.

In his second letter to Timothy, Paul stated, "I have fought the good fight, I have finished the course, I have kept the faith; in the future there is laid up for me the crown of righteousness, which the Lord, the righteous Judge, will award to me on that day; and not only to me, but also to all who have loved His appearing" (2 Tim 4:7-8 NASB). To fight a good fight and finish the course, Paul had to persevere through plenty of trials and tribulations. I am certain that you will as well. To die empty means to fulfill your calling and destiny regardless of the opposition. Absolutely nothing that we do for Christ will die with us. Every single sacrifice, hardship, accomplishment, joy, and pain is recorded in His eternal archives. When we reach the judgment seat, will Jesus say, "well done my good and faithful servant"? Or will he look at you like he did the servant who hid his talents in Matthew 25:25 and did nothing with it? There is untapped potential inside of you and God's purpose for you is to discover that well of potential.

If you are reading this book, God desires greater for you — spirit, mind and body. He desires you to walk by faith and not by sight. Walking by sight is what has made you single and anxious. However, I declare that is not your portion anymore. What lies inside of you untapped?

> *Perhaps you are wasting your life doing nothing with all you have. God packaged something in you for the good of the world — use them. We will never know the wealth God planted in you until you bring it up. There's always something in you that we haven't yet seen because that's the way God thinks. Release your ability before you die. Use the power and strength within you for the good of yourself and others. I believe there are books, songs, art works, businesses, poems, inventions and investments in you that God intended His children to enjoy. Don't give*

> *up until you have lived out the full extent of your potential, because you have no right to die with things. Don't rob the next generation of the wealth, treasure and tremendous gifts buried deep within you.* - Myles Munroe[47]

Every last one of us has something to offer to this world. The enemy loves to fight us with our own thoughts, whispering that we have nothing to offer others. We have become so accustomed to comparing our talents to others. I saw a commercial on TV One for *R&B Divas LA* and the artist Brave was being told that she had to compete with the Beyonces and Rihannas of the world.

I took a moment and thought about what a lie that was. We are told that people will not choose to buy our music or product over another because they are our competitors. That is so untrue, especially for something as inexpensive as music. People don't buy one product over another because they are better than a particular competition. People buy brands because they connect with the brand. I am an Apple user because I love the brand. I am fully invested in the company. I don't use Android because it doesn't fit my needs.

If your competition is the person next to you, that is how you will define success. The problem with this is, success in the Kingdom is not defined by our competition. Success in the kingdom is defined by the will of God. That's it. Not the will and thoughts of man. There is an ability inside of you that no other human being has. You have a gift that no one else has. When I wrote my first book *Nickey's Flesh*, I did not write it to compete, I wrote it because I had a unique story to tell. *Nickey's Flesh* wasn't on the New York Bestseller's list but it was on God's die empty list. I fought the fight and I won. I used my unique abilities to fulfill a portion of God's will for my life. *Nickey's Flesh* is the reason this is my second book and not my first. There is a journey that God has only given you that you need to empty out. The same is true when it comes to our fellowship within our local churches.

The Beauty of Community

Have you noticed that many singers and musicians discovered their talents in a local church? That isn't by coincidence. God designed the church for us to empty ourselves out. If you are a believer and not actively part of a local church, you are going to have a problem dying empty. Our gifts are designed to be used in the local church.

> *And He gave some as apostles, and some as prophets, and some as evangelists, and some as pastors and teachers, for the equipping of the saints for the work of service, to the building up of the body of Christ; until we all attain to the unity of the faith, and of the knowledge of the Son of God, to a mature man, to the measure of the stature which belongs to the fullness of Christ* (Eph. 4:11-13 NASB).

Emptiness is fully connected to God's plan for the local church. The local church is designed to use your gifts first and with the right leadership they will help you use your gifts outside of the four walls. I know that you desire to tour major platforms, climb the ladder at work, write books that are chart topping, but first, serve at your local church. A healthy local church is where your character is sharpened and you are told to wait, if needed. Our generation is likely the first generation that doesn't see the value of the local church. We believe that we know everything and know better. However, God still holds us to the standard of our gifts first being for the body of Christ.

If you are not a faithful, active member of a local church, you probably have commitment issues or you have had bad experiences in a local church. As a person who spent the last two years healing from a 10-year abusive church experience, I get it. I know the struggle of commitment. However, I also realize that all churches will not yield that same abuse and hurt. I've been a part of a new community that has embraced, loved, cared, and given us space in the community of the fellowship of God's people. All the statistics seem to point to our age being an age of "commitment-phobia." Commitment-phobia is the fear that in promising to do something good we will miss out on getting something even better.[48] But Jesus is a God of commitment. Every step that Jesus took was in commitment to His relationship with the Father. If Jesus had to be committed and accountable, what makes us any different? The apostles learned about the issues of their hearts and the authority that they walked in through their relationship with Jesus and each other. We are no different. A healthy local church is needed in order for us to heal and grow spiritually.

Our gifts are discovered when we are serving each other. In the two churches where I have held membership, both leaderships put me on the technology team. I knew that I enjoyed technology but I didn't know that I was called to it until it was put to the test in fellowship. Your gifts are not for you they are for the body of Christ.

> *If the foot says, "Because I am not a hand, I am not a part of the body," it is not for this reason any the less a part of the body. And if the ear says, "Because I am not an eye, I am not a part of the body," it is not for this reason any the less a part of the body. If the whole body were an eye, where would the hearing be? If the whole were hearing, where would the sense of smell be? But now God has placed the members, each one of them, in the body, just as He desired. If they were all one member, where would the body be? But now there are many members, but one body.*
> (1 Cor. 12:15-20 NASB)

In order for you as a single person to make an impact on this world, you need to be an active member of the body of Christ. Dying empty in your singleness requires others to sharpen your character as well as your gift. Billy Graham has a prayer he prays every morning: "Lord don't let me mess up today what took a lifetime to develop." Our giftings need to be bathed in character. If I write a book about singleness, and my character as a single was not profitable, and I am a terrible wife, why should you read it? Our characters should line up with our body of work. If you are going to die empty regarding your gifting and service, let your dying be done in a character that is proven by those who are not moved by your gifting or talents.

While there are many practical ways to die empty, I don't want you to think that dying empty means being busy. Busyness is an addiction that we use to withdraw and remain distant. Dying empty is about being purposeful with the minutes, hours, days and years the Lord has given you. You can take some time and create two bucket lists. One can be a list of all the things you would like to do for the Lord while single. The other can be all the things you have ever dreamed of doing period.

Blessings Keep Falling In My Lap

Joseph was a man who was determined to die empty regardless of what he experienced. At a young age, he had a dream that involved the purposes of his life. Joseph didn't understand that he shouldn't have shared the dream with his family members; nevertheless, his sharing the dream set him up for the promises and plans of the Lord. At times, it's hard not to share what you believe the Lord is calling you to. You should know that not everyone is going to have the excitement that you have what you are working on. Joseph experienced the hate and shade that his brothers had toward him first hand. At 17, after having a dream about one day being his brothers' leader, Joseph shared the dream with his brothers. Genesis 37 recounts that Joseph's brothers hated him because of that dream. The dream even startled his father (Jacob) who had a problem bowing down to Jacob as the dream also expressed. The brothers' hate was so deep that they plotted to kill Joseph. It was Reuben, his oldest brother, who called for them not to shed his blood, but sell him off to the Ishmaelite's instead.

Joseph's brothers did not know that the plan of God was greater than their hate. Joseph being sold into slavery was a part of God's divine plan to provide for Israel in the midst of a famine. Nowhere in Joseph's story between Genesis 37-48 does it say that Joseph complained about his situation. After being sold into slavery, he was then appointed as Pharaoh's personal servant. He had access to everything that Pharaoh owned except for his wife. Joseph knew that he could not touch Pharaoh's wife yet she tempted him anyway. When he didn't respond, she falsely accused him.

Joseph understood the plans of God. He had no idea how they were going to be fulfilled but he knew how to wait well. He didn't allow his circumstances to steer him away from what he knew the Lord called him to. Through slavery, imprisonment, being wrongly accused, back to imprisonment, he still stayed the course. Are you staying the course? Are you waiting well? Are you ready to die empty? Is your singleness worth enduring hardship?

It is important for us, whether single or married, to wait well. The first place where you should pour yourself is your family. Then your local church, community, city, and world. There have been too many dreams that God has given you that are undone. Dying empty requires intentionality. Our greatest model for what it means to die empty is Jesus Christ. When he hung on the cross, He gave up His spirit. No one was able to take it from Him. And that is how we should live. We should not be known as those who die with our greatest gifts in the grave. We are those who will die empty with nothing left in us.

It's one thing to talk about dying empty. It's another to actually live a life of persistence that isn't moved by the circumstances of life. As I've said before, being single isn't a disease, it's a gift. God has given you the gift of time to learn how to be more like him before you are joined with another. God must be enough for you. You must build a heart for God and this heart must be built on the Word of God and not all the emotions that are currently swarming around in your heart creating discontent because you aren't in a relationship or married. You are not alone. You have the Holy Spirit living inside of you. The Holy Spirit will keep your heart pure, your legs closed, and your eyes focused. Let the Lord transition your heart from bad to good in His sight.

You are the bride of Christ and you have been given a kingdom to live in! Don't allow the promise of your singleness to be wasted. God wants to give you the desires of your heart because He is the one who placed those desires in you. Then and only then will you be Single and Carefree. Being carefree doesn't mean you don't have troubles in this world. It means that you trust Jesus no matter what trouble comes your way. Allow the words from this book to guide you to a greater place in the Lord Jesus. Let it fill your greatest concern with the peace of God that passes all understanding. You can be single and not anxious! Walk worthy as a single man or woman of God who dies empty and on purpose.

AN EXERCISE IN REFLECTION

Here are some questions that my husband and I answer annually to gauge how our year is progressing. We started this practice before we were married or even courting. Our heart's desire was always to die empty as singles and be accountable for our character and gifting. Even in marriage now, this process has not stopped.

- What is your vision for this year (or remainder of the year)?
- What are the character areas you desire to work on this year?
- What do you want to accomplish physically?
- What areas of communication need to be sanctified?
- What is your personal mission statement?
- What is your life tagline (e.g. Nike's *Just Do it)?*
- What are the areas where you need to grow personally?
- What are some of your financial goals?
- What Scriptures will you focus on this year that will help you develop a godly character and lifestyle?
- How can you serve your local church better this year?
- What is the vision of your local church and can you align with it?

LOVED THE BOOK?

CHECK OUT
Single and Anxious
THE WEB SERIES at

www.singleandanxious.com

Over the course of fifteen years, *NewSeason Books and Media* has independently published thought-provoking and boundary-breaking books. We publish books in four major categories: self-help (relationships, family, leadership), spiritual resources, fiction, and memoir. In 2017, we expanded our work to include film and digital media. Our mission at NSBM is to produce transformational content and to assist all people in growing personally and spiritually.

VISIT US AT
www.newseasonbooks.com

Notes

[1] James Strong, *The Exhaustive Concordance of the Bible: Showing*
[2] Charles F. Stanley, On Holy Ground, 359 (Nashville, TN: Thomas Nelson Publishers, 1999).
[3] (2015-04-13). *Abba's Child: The Cry of the Heart for Intimate Belonging (p. 8). NavPress. Kindle Edition.*
[4] Robert G. Bratcher and William David Reyburn, *A Translator's Handbook on the Book of Psalms,* UBS Handbook Series (New York: United Bible Societies, 1991), 1052.
[5] Spiros Zodhiaates, *The Complete Word Study Dictionary: New Testament* (Chattanooga, TN: AMG Publishers, 2000).
[6] *The Holy Bible: New International Version* (Grand Rapids, MI: Zondervan, 1984), Ps 31:1.
[7] Seamands, David A.. Healing for Damaged Emotions (David Seamands Series) (Kindle Locations 445-446). David C. Cook. Kindle Edition.
[8] Goff, Bob (2012-05-01). Love Does: Discover a Secretly Incredible Life in an Ordinary World (p. 96). Thomas Nelson. Kindle Edition.
[9] Hession, Roy; Hession, Revel (2009-10-04). The Calvary Road (p. 12). Public Domain Books. Kindle Edition.
[10] Stanley, Charles (2011-03-01). Handle with Prayer: Unwrap the Source of God's Strength for Living (p. 27). David C. Cook. Kindle Edition.
[11] Stanley, Charles (2011-03-01). Handle with Prayer: Unwrap the Source of God's Strength for Living (pp. 27-28).
[12] Spiros Zodhiates, *The Complete Word Study Dictionary: New Testament* (Chattanooga, TN: AMG Publishers, 2000).
[13] John Piper, *The Dangerous Duty of Delight* (Sisters, OR: Multnomah Publishers, 2001), 21.
[14] Johannes P. Louw and Eugene Albert Nida, *Greek-English Lexicon of the New Testament: Based on Semantic Domains* (New York: United Bible Societies, 1996), 313.
[15] Tripp, Paul David (2010-03-24). What Did You Expect? (p. 33). Good News Publishers. Kindle Edition.

16 Richard Keyes, "The Idol Factory," quoted in Os Guinness and John Seel, No God but God (Chicago: Moody, 1992), 32-33.
17 Tony Evans, The Kingdom Agenda, (Evans, 257).
18 1 Cor. 1:20
19 New American Standard Bible : 1995 Update, 1 Co 1:27 (LaHabra, CA: The Lockman Foundation, 1995).
20 Yoder 17-18 Chuck Pierce
21 *New American Standard Bible: 1995 Update* (LaHabra, CA: The Lockman Foundation, 1995), 1 Co 7:32-35.
22 * All New Testament occurrences of this word are mentioned in the body of this article. Horst Robert Balz and Gerhard Schneider, *Exegetical Dictionary of the New Testament* (Grand Rapids, Mich.: Eerdmans, 1990–), 81.
23 *New American Standard Bible: 1995 Update* (LaHabra, CA: The Lockman Foundation, 1995), 1 Co 7:32-35.
24 Evans, Tony (2006-03-01). The Kingdom Agenda: What a Way to Live! (p. 263). Moody Publishers. Kindle Edition.
25 Alan F. Johnson, *1 Corinthians*, vol. 7, The IVP New Testament Commentary Series (Downers Grove, IL: InterVarsity Press, 2004), 128.
26 Mckeown, Greg (2014-04-15). Essentialism: The Disciplined Pursuit of Less (p. 206). Crown Religion/Business/Forum. Kindle Edition.
27 Manning, Brennan (2009-03-01). The Furious Longing of God (p. 38). David C. Cook. Kindle Edition.
28 Allen C. Myers, *The Eerdmans Bible Dictionary* (Grand Rapids, MI: Eerdmans, 1987), 846.
29 Stanley, Charles (2011-03-01). Handle with Prayer: Unwrap the Source of God's Strength for Living (p. 24). David C. Cook. Kindle Edition.
30 Allen C. Myers, *The Eerdmans Bible Dictionary* (Grand Rapids, MI: Eerdmans, 1987), 846.
31 David Watson, *Called and Committed* (Wheaton, Ill: Harold Shaw Publishers, 1982), 103.
32 Spiros Zodhiates, *The Complete Word Study Dictionary: New Testament* (Chattanooga, TN: AMG Publishers, 2000).

[33] Hendricks, William D.; Howard G. G. Hendricks; William D. Hendricks; Howard G. Hendricks (2007-05-01). Living By the Book/Living By the Book Workbook Set (Kindle Locations 2094-2097). Moody Publishers. Kindle Edition.
[34] Spiros Zodhiates, *The Complete Word Study Dictionary: New Testament* (Chattanooga, TN: AMG Publishers, 2000).
[35] David Watson, *Called and Committed* (Wheaton, Ill: Harold Shaw Publishers, 1982), 193.
[36] Spiros Zodhiates, *The Complete Word Study Dictionary: New Testament* (Chattanooga, TN: AMG Publishers, 2000).
[37] Spiros Zodhiates, *The Complete Word Study Dictionary: New Testament* (Chattanooga, TN: AMG Publishers, 2000).
[38] Spiros Zodhiates, *The Complete Word Study Dictionary: New Testament* (Chattanooga, TN: AMG Publishers, 2000).
[39] Ryken, Philip Graham (2012-01-31). Loving the Way Jesus Loves (p. 19). Crossway. Kindle Edition.
[40] Ryken, Philip Graham (2012-01-31). Loving the Way Jesus Loves (p. 57). Crossway. Kindle Edition.
[41] Ryken, Philip Graham (2012-01-31). Loving the Way Jesus Loves (p. 101). Crossway. Kindle Edition.
[42] Lomas, David; Jacobsen, D. R. (2014-02-01). The Truest Thing about You: Identity, Desire, and Why It All Matters (Kindle Locations 163-164). David C. Cook. Kindle Edition
[43] Spiros Zodhiates, *The Complete Word Study Dictionary: New Testament* (Chattanooga, TN: AMG Publishers, 2000).
[44] *New American Standard Bible: 1995 Update* (LaHabra, CA: The Lockman Foundation, 1995),.
[45] Goff, Bob (2012-05-01). Love Does: Discover a Secretly Incredible Life in an Ordinary World (p. 31). Thomas Nelson. Kindle Edition.
[46] Spiros Zodhiates, *The Complete Word Study Dictionary: New Testament* (Chattanooga, TN: AMG Publishers, 2000).
[47] Munroe, Myles. *Understanding Your Potential: Discovering the Hidden You*. Bahamas: Destiny Image Publishers, Inc., 1991.
[48] Dever, Mark (2004-09-30). Nine Marks of a Healthy Church (p. 147). Good News Publishers/Crossway Books. Kindle Edition.

www.ingramcontent.com/pod-product-compliance
Lightning Source LLC
Chambersburg PA
CBHW031420290426
44110CB00011B/465